Our Emotions and Culture

Our Emotions and Culture

How Modern Life Changes Us

E. Doyle McCarthy

ANTHEM PRESS

Anthem Press
An imprint of Wimbledon Publishing Company
www.anthempress.com

This edition first published in UK and USA 2025
by ANTHEM PRESS
75–76 Blackfriars Road, London SE1 8HA, UK
or PO Box 9779, London SW19 7ZG, UK
and
244 Madison Ave #116, New York, NY 10016, USA

© 2025 E Doyle McCarthy

British Library Cataloguing-in-Publication Data
A catalogue record for this book is available from the British Library.

Library of Congress Cataloging-in-Publication Data: 2024943668
A catalog record for this book has been requested.

ISBN-13: 978-1-83998-073-2 (Hbk)/ 978-1-83998-076-3 (Pbk)
ISBN-10: 1-83998-073-7 (Hbk) / 1-83998-076-1 (Pbk)

This title is also available as an e-book.

CONTENTS

For JJH

PREFACE

"Not only ideas, but emotions too, are cultural artifacts…."
— Clifford Geertz, *The Interpretation of Cultures*

A lot of us know what emotions are or we think we do. And we also know a lot about culture, perhaps we know about our own US culture, but we might think that other people really "have" culture, not us. But this idea and set of attitudes that "others have culture, not us!" is a wrongheaded idea; it is even highly prejudicial, as I will argue here briefly and in a nutshell: *Every group of people who have lived in the same place and who share a history have something in common with others with whom they live. We call that thing that people share "culture."* Like the US people share things in common—it is that simple. We share our geography and we share events, past and present, and we share our particular history and we share the history and the lives of the various peoples and groups who live here now and in the past; these groups have left their mark on us all, good or bad, old groups and new ones too.

Despite all the ways that many of us understand our country and its culture, we can easily get these things right or wrong; maybe we think about these matters clearly, but we often do so with judgments and prejudices, and these judgments shape our thinking about these difficult matters—I mean the difficult understandings we have about what a group of people is really like. This is also a matter of how we ourselves belong to our group, what we call our Identity.

Even when we consider today's post-pandemic conflicts and difficulties with politics, crime and violence, and other inequities, people today seem to use the word "culture" a lot in our everyday lives, or we hear others use it a lot. *This book is intended to develop and refine and, maybe, change what we know about these two things—culture and emotion.* My argument briefly is that our feelings and emotions are important parts of our culture, now and in the past. But I will also argue that in today's world, our feelings and emotions have become possessions of great value to many of us. To put it simply: we live in an Emotional Age.

I would guess that when it comes to emotions—our own and others—we do not think about our feelings and emotions as part of culture. *By culture, I mean that shared system or collection of the meanings we give to various things,* like mothers, sailors, birthday cakes, or the Vietnam War Memorial—to think of some examples. These meanings are contained and transmitted in words, in things like food and dress, in ceremonies we perform, and in the ways we have fun and pursue pleasure. Each of these parts of a group or society of people contains the meanings we give to them, like the forms of respect and affection we give parents, or how we think of sailors as people who are adventurous and brave, if a bit disreputable. Or, we think of war memorials as places to remember and to honor the war dead and to honor the nation at the same time. The meanings we give to all kinds of things are contained in what we think and how we act and, yes, what we feel. So *culture is more than just a collection of ideas or beliefs located in our heads. It is also a part of what we do or how we act and how we feel about everything in our social worlds, including our emotions.* So being a parent means doing things and feeling things that parents are expected to do and to feel; when we go to a war memorial, most of us know, instinctively, how to act and what we are supposed to feel at these memorials. In doing and acting these ways, we are drawing from our culture, our ideas and beliefs as well as what feelings or dress or behavior others like us have come to associate with the particular situation we are in.

To state this briefly*: the central idea of this book is that emotions are part of culture too; there are many social meanings about what emotions are and how and whether to express them or not.*

An important part of understanding how people's lives are shaped by their culture is to understand the many people and places that shape what we think and feel about the meaning of things. We could call them "influencers," today's word that comes from the world of entertainment and advertising and social media. Influencers are those people and organizations who are thought to have an expert level of knowledge about something (cosmetics, health, fashion, food, parenting, etc.). Influencers can shape people's buying and consuming habits in various ways, like posting photos, videos, or messages online.

Another word is even more basic than the word "influencers"; the word I am thinking of is a word that comes from sociology; it is *authority*—referring to those people who are regarded as having the right to tell us what to believe and what we are supposed to think about something. I am thinking, for example, of the authority of rabbis, teachers, grandmothers, US presidents, and federal judges, but also the corner druggist. Each of these people is viewed as having the right ("legitimacy" is another word for this) to tell us how to act and what to think and do in the various places we travel in everyday life; there are those who tell us what to do at work, at home, when we are with our friends as well as those "friends" we watch on media news shows or sitcoms or talk shows. The druggist might tell us if we should take a certain medication and what effects to watch for, if we take it. In general, the role of an authority is important in shaping our lives today and in shaping what we actually think and feel and also what we think we are *supposed to think and feel and do* about this or that.

One central question of this book is *what are the meanings we give to our emotions and where do these meanings come from* and who are the authorities, if any, that we think we are supposed to listen to about our feelings and emotions? Authorities carry a lot of weight in shaping what we think and do and what we feel too.

To conclude this brief Preface, I also want to say here that this topic of emotions is very close to me for many reasons. For one, I have thought, for some time now, that today we live in an Emotional Age and that navigating today's world means understanding a lot about emotions, our own but also understanding how our emotions are shaped by others.

This idea has brought me into many conflicts with the way I was brought up in the 1950s. At that time, being controlled and disciplined was valued even for children and teens and certainly adults; being emotional was not valued by most people in most settings. In fact, it was a mark of a "grown-up" person that you were supposed to be a "nice" person and controlled about anything emotional that you felt like anger or jealousy or even any of the types of pleasures surrounding you, like food or sex or comfort. If you felt strongly about these things, you were careful not to talk about it. Not today.

Things have changed! We and others talk a lot about what we feel and how we feel. We talk about and watch a lot of sex, some of it is regarded as "pornography," while other types of sex are seen simply as "entertainment." We watch people—on screens or in person—cook and eat and talk about the dishes they love to eat. We ourselves seek out places and people we enjoy or that give us pleasure. We are filled with oral cravings and forbidden and secret desires. We watch with pleasure all kinds of sports and games that show us highly skilled types of violence and aggression. We also prefer that these athletes speak about their games in unemotional or matter-of-fact tones.

Here are some other examples that are close to me: the TV commercials I watch today shock me a little because they are far more emotional than in earlier decades of my life. Buying and selling things today—online or in stores—involves each of us getting worked up or excited emotionally. Advertisers ask: "Do these goods, from clothes to chocolate cookies, make people feel better or even excited? Or do they make us feel comfortable?"

I am saying here that many of the things we use and buy serve as signs of other things, as signs of emotional happiness or success or being cool;

things—from clothes to lipstick or cologne—can serve as signs of ourselves, our *identities*. Material things that we use and adorn are "semiotic"—a word that means that things and people can serve as signs or signifiers of beauty, success, being cool, being a real American, and so forth.

Some people today even say that our feelings and emotions operate, for us and for others, as types of authority, telling us what to do and how to think, even more than governmental authorities or even our elders do. And then there is also our lives on what is called Social Media—Facebook, Twitter, Instagram, and Snapchat—that also and often appeal to our emotions, like my desires or fears or my anger or my nostalgic feeling about something (the role of media today I discuss in Chapter 5). Politics too has also become much more openly emotional today compared to decades ago.

This book is written to try to understand this complex world we live in today, an Emotional World.

A brief note on the form of this book: this is a short book, written in a popular and accessible style, about how emotions are important to the everyday lives of people who live in "modern" and "postmodern" societies. The model for this book and its references was set by Peter L. Berger and his best-selling *Invitation to Sociology*. I share Berger's conviction—taken from the sociology of knowledge—that my own analysis of emotions is a peculiarly modern and timely form of critical thought.

I have tried in the final chapter, Chapter 6, to explain what I mean by "critical thought."

The final section, Sources and Further Readings, provides sources, chapter by chapter.

Chapter 1

INTRODUCTION: ON
INDIVIDUALISM AND EMOTIONS

We Americans—and this crosses classes and ethnic/racial groups too—have a long and distinguished history of respecting the value called *individualism*, the idea of the solitary and autonomous, self-sufficient human person, and the idea that each and all of these persons are equal both in moral and social terms. While the word "individualism" has had many meanings, especially across different peoples and nations, in the United States it has stood for America's idea of itself as a land and a people where individuals matter and where people are self-reliant as opposed to working together with social groups and classes to accomplish our goals. Individualism in the United States is a word and an idea that originated in the nineteenth century, although its roots go back to when the Puritans settled in the United States in the seventeenth century. As individualist ideas and values settled in America, individualism developed closely with the belief in the American Dream of the equal opportunity of individuals and the modern idea of the nation as a collectivity of equal individuals. A country that is individualistic is focused on the values of individuals over those of collectivity. Put differently, it is a society where "I" dominates the "We."

Among individualism's many meanings, Americans have *believed that we achieve what we do because of our individual skills and our individual talents and drives.* We have often referred to this as being "self-made" men and women. Because of this, we tend to respect and follow those who show their achievements—which we regard as *individual* achievements—through wealth, fame, and success. And, unlike other peoples, we tend to see poor people as having only themselves to blame for their plight. After all, poor people are individuals too! This is why poor people show many of us what personal failure looks like. And, on the flip side, the same goes for the rich and famous who have shown many of us what individual success looks like. These ideas are still with us today although, admittedly, they take different forms in different peoples and places in America right now. These ideas are also great sources of conflict in communities of many kinds (e.g., religious, familial, ethnic, racial, rich, vs.

poor communities) and in national politics. For example, Americans tend, even today, to place a great deal of value on helping others in need. This seems to belie the value of rugged individualism; in other words, caring for others is a shared value that some see as in tension with our rugged individualism. This opens up the question: Do we Americans think of helping our neighbors in need as consistent with our individualism? Or not?—a good topic for discussion.

Here is a quick summary of the meanings of American individualism:

- ...to be individualist means to value autonomy,
- ...to value independence,
- ...to value self-reliance,
- ...to value a person who is "self-made."

Now, I want to consider with you the topic of emotions and individualism. Simply put, most of us most of the time think that *emotions belong to each of us*, meaning that they principally tell us something important about us *as individuals*: so we say that someone is a sensitive person with deep feelings or that she is in touch with her feelings; these descriptions tend to be positive evaluations. Or, to use another example, we might say that someone is weird, or a jerk or a creep, because she only thinks about herself and has no feelings for others. In other words, many of us tend to think *that emotions express something deeply personal and individual* and important, even something real and authentic, about each of us and about our character as an individual. So we mostly think that our feelings and emotions are principally *mine or yours*—my sadness and joy, my particular political ideas and feelings, my motives and aspirations, and my desires—these are all expressions of *me*, the self I really am.

These ideas are shared by so many of us that they seem to be obviously true: *Emotions are the experiences of the individual self.* Here is a brief statement of a business psychologist in a newspaper editorial opinion column. The author, a prominent psychologist whose work I recommend for discussion (see citation 8 for Chapter 1), argues for a social understanding of emotions.

I paraphrase what he wrote:

Most people view emotions as existing in their heads or in their own bodies, whether shame, embarrassment, joy, or sadness, for example. Happiness is thought of as an individual state of mind. Melancholy is an indicator of a person's mental illness. But the truth is that emotions are, in many important ways, *social*. Emotions are vital parts of our interactions with others. In fact, we are emotional precisely because we have interacted with others and learned from these interactions what our emotions mean.

The main idea of this book is to think about emotions this way, as social in many important respects. I do not want to argue that emotions are not individual aspects of each of us. Clearly, they are, and in important ways too. Rather, I want to make the argument that emotions are also important aspects of us as social beings and that our culture shapes our emotions—all of our emotions—in important ways. In other words, others are important for what we feel and how we feel. Take isolation from others. It generates feelings of despair or depression or anxiety in us. This may be because others are so important to us.

Others and society itself shape and have shaped our experiences including our emotional experiences—what we feel, how we talk about how we feel, what feelings and emotions *mean to us*, whether we allow ourselves to express our feelings or not, and what these feelings mean to us or say to us. There are many ways that other people, society, and culture shape our emotions and our reactions to our own emotions and our reactions to others' emotions too.

So, for example, we might ask questions like these. Each of these questions implies that people place social values on their emotions and they are aware of the values that others place on these emotions:

1. "Is anger a good thing or not?"
2. "Should I act on my desires for a close relationship with another person? Or, "Should I keep these feelings to myself?"
3. "Should I show or hide, express or repress, the feelings I have about women or Black people?"
4. "If I show or express these feelings, am I at risk of disapproval or rejection from others?"
5. Or maybe we say, "We don't care what others think of us," even knowing that we might have to face rejection or disapproval from them. This also shows us that what we feel about our feelings is, in important ways, shaped by others and "society." In some cases, for example, in being open about our feelings and emotions we might suffer the consequences of hatred, ostracism, or social isolation from others. This can show us how much emotions and emotional expressions matter both to us and to others too. Emotions, many of us believe, carry important social meanings about people. Emotional expressions, to use another example, are like a kind of social language that tells others (and we tell ourselves too) who we are and the kind of person we are or want to be.

To put it simply, each of these examples (1–5 above) can show us how much our feelings and emotions—like comfort or discomfort about our feelings and desires, for example, or about our anger, shame, sympathy, or disgust—are shaped by our *beliefs* about these feelings and emotions. These beliefs come from "society."

Let me explain what I mean, using the example of anger:

ANGER: Concerning question 1: most of us are aware that the emotion we call "anger" can be good or bad depending on the situation as well as the status of the person who is angry, as well as the person or thing that is the object of our anger. These social rules about anger and being angry are set by society: so, a lot of people think that men are typically allowed to express anger more often than women or that higher status people are allowed to express anger more than those of lower status people, like students, clients, or workers who are supposed to be more obedient or respectful of their bosses or "social superiors." This clearly suggests that there are social rules or norms about being angry, expressing anger, and the situation we might be in and what that situation calls for. For example, I might feel anger toward the physician I consult, but I do not think that I would dare to express it. Or, I might be afraid of my doctor, but not express it or speak of it for fear that she might take it out on me in some way. Or, I might not want her to think badly of me.

These examples bring up something else: we might correctly fear the reactions of those we are physically close to or those we are emotionally close to, since in either situation the other might be able to harm us in some way. Whereas those we are distanced from or remote from we don't typically perceive as physical or emotional threats to us.

Here is a recent statement about controlling anger in social situations. It is taken from a course that teaches people the *social meanings of being angry or controlling anger*:

It is taken from an online Anger Management Course (see citation 9 for Chapter 1):

> Controlling and limiting anger is important in every aspect of one's life. Without control you are putting limits on what you can accomplish. Anger can be an incredibly damaging force, costing people their jobs, and personal relationships. However, since everyone experiences anger, having a constructive approach to manage it effectively can turn it into a valuable asset.

So, as we can see from this example, people who take this course are being taught rules about the meaning of anger: Anger can be a dangerous thing; or, anger expressed correctly can be a healthy and productive thing. But there is even more to the emotion we call anger than this.

Over time, in the modern period (discussed fully in Chapter 2) of roughly the last 500 years in places like North America and Europe, people's ideas about anger have changed quite a lot. To put this simply and to describe something fairly recent, what we call "culture"—in this case, the ideas and meanings we have given to anger—have changed for different generations and groups of Americans, and this pertains to Canada, the UK, and to many European nations too. So when we think and talk about anger, I am saying that our ideas about the meanings of anger have changed a lot over this long period of time, since the seventeenth century, say.

For example, in the United States of the nineteenth century and into the early decades of the twentieth century, anger was almost always negatively regarded, and people were expected to control their anger and to teach their children to do so too. Whereas today, when emotions have become something more of us are taught to both cultivate and express, there is a new standard or "culture" that asserts the value of getting in touch with our anger and even knowing how and when to express it and how to manage our anger; these abilities are regarded today as "healthy." The quote above on Anger Management shows us this current view, one that is familiar to many of us, old and young. I should add something else about anger and how it is managed: those of us who fail at managing our anger—like men who beat women, those who engage in "road rage," teachers who handle children with too much strictness and punishment, or salespeople who get angry at their customers—might end up having to take an "Anger Management Course," where they are instructed on ways to handle their own anger and others' anger too. There are plenty of these courses online! Try "Googling" them. On these sites, you can read about the best therapies for anger management and the stages of anger management too.

One more thing about emotions and change. Many scholars have argued that our current culture demands much more of each of us than our pre-decessors. They say this because, by today's standards and culture, we are supposed to understand our own and others' emotions in order to control or to express these feelings and to help us engage with others in many social set-tings. In the business world of today, for example, there is even a best-selling book and videos on YouTube that teach people how we have to be smart or intelligent about emotions in order to succeed in business today. There is a best-selling book, published in 2005, called *Emotional* Intelligence: *Why It Can Matter More Than IQ.* This book argues that each of us needs to be emotionally intelligent in order to succeed in the many aspects of our lives, jobs, intimate relations, raising children, and so forth (see citation 10 for Chapter 1 notes).

Here is what one researcher, an historian, wrote about today's standards about emotions. I paraphrase:

Americans today, on the whole, follow the standard of being open about our feelings and emotions. Many of us also accept people's emotions and their own emotional reactions as part of reality itself. There is evidence that emotions are looked upon in positive terms today (in contrast with the past), as important aspects of our identities (see citation 11 for Chapter 1).

This historian agrees with that psychologist who wrote that while many of us think about emotions as existing in our heads. In reality, emotions are social for they are an important part of our social interactions.

The fact that the meanings of emotions change over time in the same societies suggests that emotional experiences and what emotions mean to us are something more than an individual matter. It is also collective and social or cultural. The meanings of emotions are something we share with others. Otherwise, we could not understand each other or read what our own emotions might be telling us about ourselves or others—sometimes good things; other times, emotions can tell us bad or difficult things about ourselves, or our emotions might tell us things in need of correction. In the book that follows, I plan to take us through some of these arguments about *emotions as social things*, shaped by culture.

In conclusion, let me summarize my main points here: whatever we think about emotions, emotions are also—inescapably and in important ways—cultural objects, however much we know and feel them "as our own" (or as someone else's). Put differently, *emotions are social things because we share their meanings with others. Emotions belong to the entire domain of culture and human meaning.* But let me now get on with the business of advancing this argument.

In the next chapter (Chapter 2), we will talk about the idea and the concept of the modern world or "modernity." This idea was created to help observers like me organize and study and interpret the real-time changes in societies of the last 400–500 years in Europe and North America—the rise of science and technologies, the mobility of populations, the rise of cities, and the new forms of modern art and culture. Today, the entire world is described as undergoing major changes like these; world peoples today expect to be undergoing profound changes in both their societies and in themselves, arguments that we will review in Chapter 2.

Chapter 3 discusses the leading idea in emotion science of "emotional culture." This refers to a collective and shared set of ideas and practices (or, things we do) about what emotions are and how they are experienced and what they mean.

In Chapter 4, I will discuss some ideas about the shaping of the Social Self today and how today Identity has become closely associated with Authenticity and its pursuit; this idea and value of authenticity is about a real self or a natural self that we want to get in contact with. We often contrast this authentic self to the self of our everyday dramas, roles, and performances. Or we contrast authenticity with social life itself and the roles we are forced to play in our everyday lives. In this chapter, I want to open up some questions about the social meanings of authenticity today.

In Chapter 5, we will consider how late modern life, especially global capitalism and mass media today, has shaped our emotions and made us more emotional compared to our predecessors. We will also consider how public life today has become a place where we anticipate and search out emotional happenings: at shopping malls, concerts, sports events and political rallies, and at memorials for people lost to death and disaster, whether on city streets or at sites of natural disasters, or at any site where someone was killed.

In the concluding chapter, Chapter 6, we sum up our arguments and consider with our readers what all these emotions mean for us today. Are we drawn to the many ways and sites where we can feel things intensely? Do these feelings help to divide us or to unite us? What can we make of all the emotional dramas that fill up our lives and our yearnings? Has media, in its various forms, changed us or not? These questions can be used for discussions of Chapter 1.

Today, we seem to seek out emotions in the many places and stages of our lives: the malls where we walk and dance to the rhythms of packaged background Musak and music played in elevators, retail stores, and other public establishments; the concerts we attend as spectators-participants; the city parks that provide walkways for us to parade with others; the church gatherings where we discover our faith and where we connect with others with whom we sing and weep. What does all this emotion mean, and where is this new emotional culture taking us, and where will this take us into the future? These are my questions. I hope these are your questions as well.

Chapter 2

WHAT IS MODERNITY?
HOW THE MODERN WORLD
SHAPED OUR EMOTIONS?

The idea as well as the very concept of the modern world or "modernity" that I invoked in Chapter 1 is one argued about and criticized by many scholars in the social sciences and humanities today. In fact, these arguments and discussions go back to the classic works in sociology, written in the years 1890–1930. In these works—read today from whatever place we occupy in the modern world—modernity is a world that overwhelms us with its complexities and with the vastness of its bureaucratic institutions and its capitalist economy. But it is also true that modernity has given to modern peoples—and certainly given to some of us more than to others—both their actual freedoms and their experiences of freedom and release or liberation from others, from groups, and from society itself.

On the flip side, the modern world has fostered in many of us experiences of being separate or alone and alienated from others and our society. This has created a disconnect between who we are and what our society is. Put differently, many modern people suffer from an ongoing and irresolute "identity crisis," resulting from the lack of symmetry or harmony or balance between who I am and what society is. In fact, earlier societies (ones we could label premodern or traditional societies) fostered a kind of integration or harmony of self and society where, especially, faith and other powerful forces like the authority of kings and princes connected each of us to the natural and social order, where individual people belonged to a hierarchical or stratified universe that reached from their ordinary daily lives to the heavens—that place where divinities reside, a place of god or gods, angels, saints, and so forth.

What I have just described is sometimes called the "great chain of being," uniting each of us with the religious universe where we reside, creating a sense of us being at home both in our skin and in the universe itself. By contrast, modern people like us have been said to suffer from a permanent condition of homelessness, of not belonging anywhere in any final sense. Another way of describing this homelessness is to point to a problem modern people share, their identity—who am I anyway? In the Sources and Further Readings section at the end of this book, readers are invited to enter these discussions about modernity, important ones even today.

Depending on the field and its approach, "modernity" may refer to different time periods running from the fourteenth-century Renaissance, marking the end of Europe's Middle Ages, through either the mid-twentieth century or to the end of World War I, November 11, 1918. Or "modern" might also be used to refer to the broad and shared characteristics of these societies and their inhabitants today, from changes in food and clothing and art and architecture to its forms of technological war-making or to people's shared experiences, such as their beliefs in freedom, both personal and political freedom. In other words, "modern" can mean many things, but those like me who use this term usually refer to the big changes in people themselves and in those societies that underwent changes in the first age of industrial capitalism that spanned the nineteenth to the mid-twentieth centuries.

The changes of the first modern world typically refer to big changes like the early inventions of science and technology in the sixteenth and seventeenth centuries, or the introduction of industry into production and travel at the same time, or bringing new tools and inventions into farms and households, or the new ways of transporting peoples across land and other spaces, or the invention of elevators without which cities and tall buildings could not develop, or new forms of communication, for example, printing presses for modern newspapers followed by technologies where transmission was simultaneous, like telegraphs or telephones.

In this book, I understand the modern world as a set of leading ideas and *discourses* about the social and economic changes ushered in hundreds of years ago in the West, things like the rise of modern cities, the rise of the new capitalist economy, and the rise of modern democracies. By modern "discourse" I mean the meaning of things, in words and in concepts, that belong to particular modern institutions that were ushered in with the modern world, like social science, psychiatry, the arts, government, or university. Here are some examples of changing modern discourses: new types of thinking and doing things like modern therapies (psychology and psychiatry); print journalism (the rise of newspapers and books) and digital (online) journalism; new forms of writing like the personal essay or the novel; the speeches of public figures; and everyday forms of speaking and expressing oneself.

The idea and discourse of modernity—what it was and when it happened—was created to help academic observers like me to organize and to study and to interpret the real-time changes in societies and peoples of the last 400–500 years in Europe and North America, especially the rise of industrial capitalism but also the many social changes associated with capitalism, like cities and new technologies as well as more recent forms of marketing and consuming and branding in the world of today's industrial capitalism.

Things like industry and markets and their class structures are associated with the first modern world originating, some say, about the year 1600 around the period of the Protestant Reformation that ushered a set of ideas conducive to the generation of capitalism and its pursuits. This early modern period also brought with it greater social and political freedoms for some; it also introduced a collective and newly emerging sense of the right and freedom for some individuals to believe and to worship (or not) their own god in a freely chosen religious community with others. Before this religious revolution, there was one dominant and dominating Christian faith throughout the Middle Ages, united by the rule of the church and the papacy in Rome. The Holy Roman Empire refers to the most powerful European political state of the Middle Ages. Its rule—by the Roman Church and emperors—ended in the modern era in 1806 with the end of the Napoleonic Wars. Since the nineteenth century, modern societies are made up of a multiplicity of modern nation-states.

But we cannot forget that the word "modern" was also used—ideologically—as both word and concept to justify modern nations' own power and superiority relative to other world peoples. So the "modern" world as it was written and spoken was a type of weapon to wield power in its own societies and in the world at large, against peoples near and far, against nations and peoples foreign and remote, and certainly against peoples of non-white and non-Christian races, ethnicities, and nationalities, for example. In other words, for all its advancements in democracy and in the freedom of individuals and groups, the modern world was a world that developed simultaneously with colonialism, imperialism, and multiple forms of slavery as well as sexism (a word developed about a prejudice of men that some considered as important as racism).

Everything that modern people did and wrote about their lives, the ways they accomplished things—in the sciences, in arts, and in politics—displayed a new sense of themselves and their worlds; many people call those things "modern," because they never existed before. They were modern. They were new.

To cite some more neutral examples of modernism: works of fiction called "novels" are viewed by many scholars today as distinctly modern "realist" forms of writing, focusing on the everyday lives of ordinary people. These novels—Gustave Flaubert's novel *Madame Bovary* is considered a seminal work of modern literary realism—represented a self-conscious break with traditional ways of writing; they were, in this sense, experiments with new literary forms and expressions. Another example from the arts: Jazz music, considered distinctly modern in form, departed from chords and used improvisation in playing, its roots in Blues and Ragtime, dating back in the United States to the late nineteenth and early twentieth century.

Modern Experiences of Self and Society

For our purposes here, writing about emotions, my interest is in the ways people's experiences of yesterday and today are distinctly "modern," meaning that these experiences are relatively new on the human scene, the shape or form of our experiences. By this I also mean that our experiences today are only a few hundred years in the making. So, these human beings of recent vintage—ourselves—share experiences and attitudes that we call modern or postmodern or late modern: more specifically, *they/we tend to think of ourselves as individuals, as separate and apart from others and society itself; we have questions about who we are and are subject to "identity crises"; we are subject to loneliness and anxieties; privacy is important to us as our families are, in many ways, important to us, just as both of these are experienced as burdens to many of us.*

All of this suggests that modernization puts into motion a new social world where people expect all kinds of changes in their societies and themselves: changes like industrialization and technical development; changes like these occur again and again in the modern world; and people *themselves* are and expect to be more mobile and changeable than peoples who lived in the societies of yesteryear.

If "modernity" means anything useful and even important—and I think it does—it serves as a description of a process human beings have lived through and still live through, *a sequence of events that changed and still change a simpler and traditional way of life, stable and contained, and, in many instances, a social hierarchy made legitimate or justified by religion and tradition into a new kind of social world where strangers work and live side-by-side with strangers.* In fact, one anthropologist has described this new modern world as a place where people, for the first time, lived and worked among strangers, people unknown to them.

So allow me to state my argument again: a lasting trait of modern societies of yesteryear and today is that of the *transformation of persons themselves*—their experiences and their identities—that go hand-in-hand with the transformations of their worlds. Put differently, these social changes clearly get under our skin; for they render both us and our worlds changeable and unstable, however much they hold out promises of change for a better life and a better world. Modern people live with disintegration and improvement, and rupture and integration; we move and we settle, for a time. Modernity unsettles us,

again and again, while carrying us along with promises of a better and hap-
pier life for us and for others. Clearly, all of this uncertainty reverberates emotionally, making us more open to change but more anxious and unsettled too.

This points to the rise of a new type of person—a modern "individual" discussed in Chapter 1, a person who is autonomous and not tied down to others
and to society itself, a person whose experiences include an intense sense of
one's own changing reality. The very meaning of "individual" or "individuality" means the person who I am irrespective of the social roles I occupy and
the functions I perform. I am a person "in my own right"; modern individuals
are a kind of absolute without reference to those groups to which they belong.
Some writers describe it this way:

> *My reality stands above all others; it is the only one that counts; my subjectivity or my
> experience of myself can also exist in conflict or tension with how I imagine "society"
> and its institutions.*

The modern world has also introduced new and distinctive attitudes and dis-
positions about what it is to have an emotional life today. I am thinking of
many things, like these: first, our preoccupation today with and attention to
feelings and emotions, dating back to the seventeenth century, that we find in
the writings of modern philosophers like René Descartes; second, our shared
lack of trust in each other and in today's institutions and our lack of trust in
reason and science itself. This suggests that today, older forms of authority
over us—princes or presidents, governments and their laws, and experts of
all kinds—no longer have legitimate claims over us individuals. We typically
believe that we answer to our own dictates as to what to do and how to live.
Each of us is its own authority.

But what needs much more explanation is my claim that modern persons today have become more emotional, even seeking out occasions for the
experience of intense emotions. Ours is a time of emotional overload, both a
form of emotional saturation and a time of emotional emancipation or freedom, each with different but related social sources. This is a good discussion topic—emotional overload—to explore using some of our readings (see
Sources and Further Readings section). But how did this Emotional World
come about?

In order to proceed with an account of modern emotionality, I will link
it directly to the problem of modern identity, *asking how the emotions became so
central to us today living in the ages of modernity.* One way to study this is to draw
from historians and other scholars writing on this topic of modern emotionality. Here is a brief summary of what they have found: they have studied the
rise of the Romantic Movement of the late eighteenth century and, at its peak

from 1800 to 1850, a movement seen by many as a major revolt against the formidable eighteenth-century Age of Reason and Science.

Romanticism—its discovery of nature brimming with the power of life itself—found expression in different ways, influencing eighteenth- and nineteenth-century social life and culture, its *politics* (the rise of the people's democracies and nationalisms) and its intensely felt social movements for equity and justice; its romantic and sentimental *novels*; and its *art* including its intensely sentimental (i.e., suffused with emotion) portraits of animals, children, landscapes, and wilderness. *Romanticism's central theme was the problem of subjectivity or self-consciousness, as a way to interpret and to understand the vitality and intensity of a person's subjective imagination and consciousness.*

Scholars argue that Romanticism has left its mark on today's modern and late modern culture, with its emphasis on spontaneity, intensity, and authenticity (Chapter 4). Perhaps most important was the romantic idea that *within each of us* nature can be experienced and known. In other words, the modern self or subject has as a primary disposition, an *inwardness,* a new social space, and a world of inner objects like emotions and experiences. Sentiment became important as feeling became a person's way of reaching nature itself, located deep within oneself. Nature is the voice within us, as Jean-Jacques Rousseau first argued.

The meaning of today's emotions, believed to be sources of our liberation from society and from ourselves, may, if these historians are correct, have its roots in the older Romantic belief of the power of our feelings and emotions to bring us freedom and an authentic life. Today's emotions, while shaped by our modern histories, have taken on new social meanings today and belong to a newer emotional culture (Chapter 3), one that is distinctly our own, its emphasis found in several keywords: self, identity, experience, freedom, authenticity, psychology, pleasure, culture, and nature. It is to that, more recent, history and culture that I now turn.

Chapter 3

EMOTIONAL CULTURES: UNDERSTANDING THE CONCEPT

Those who study emotions argue that *what emotions mean* is an important part of any *culture*. To paraphrase the famous anthropologist Clifford Geertz: *Not only ideas but emotions too are cultural things; the meanings of various emotions are learned in society and, especially, in interactions with others.* Let us hold that thought—emotions are cultural things—as we go through this chapter together.

Emotions can mean many things: to put it simply, in one society *being emotional* might mean that a person is a good or bad person, whether a person of humble status or an elite. Today, emotional expressions of intense anger might mean that a person lacks self-control and/or might even be a danger to others or to herself. Emotions, accompanied by tears, might indicate that someone is highly sensitive and sympathetic to the plight of others but, clearly, tears are read differently for women versus men or emotions surely mean different things for one's mother versus one's boss. Emotions like anger, if directed toward groups regarded as oppressors, might be perceived by some groups as justified and as a good resource for egalitarian political movements. Emotions, like language, also *speak to us* about the worth or the status of a person or group. So, to study emotions means that we should examine the shared or collective ideas about what feelings and emotions mean to various peoples, how they are read or perceived by them. This is what emotional cultures tell us, *what emotions mean*, for us and for others.

As part of an emotional culture is expression, how and whether emotions are expressed at all. For example, should most of our intense feelings and emotions—anger, pleasure, sadness, shame, or embarrassment—be controlled and un-expressed or is it better (socially preferred) to express emotions openly to others and to ourselves? To cite one example from the United States, not long ago middle-class people were raised to avoid speaking about or commenting about the food they were eating, whether they liked it or not, or whether it tasted good or bad. To do so was "vulgar" or "crass," or it revealed something lacking in one's upbringing. Today in the United States, many of us can and do speak openly and freely about the food we eat and want to eat or the food we crave. There is even a word today for people who openly proclaim their love of food and eating and who have a great interest in food, its procurement, and its preparation. The word "Foodies" appeared in print for the first time in the 1980s. Among its many meanings, the word foodie refers, positively, to anyone, a common person like you or me, and certainly not a member of an elite group like a "gourmand" or "gastronome." A foodie is one who claims to love food and eating, including its purchase and preparation and serving. Most importantly, anyone can claim to be a foodie as foodies are not considered either specialists or elites.

To use a very different example, if we are persons who are restrained about what we are feeling or sensing or if we are "cool" about revealing our feelings to others, we might risk being negatively labeled today as a difficult person, even cold or indifferent or uptight or over-controlling about our emotions and others' emotions too; we might even be called "control freaks," a negative word, meaning that we are overly concerned about controlling the emotions and behaviors of ourselves and others. Today, being a "control freak" is always a negative judgment of a person. On the other hand, if we are seen to be "cool," this might mean something good or positive about us; maybe it matters whether this label or assessment of us is with close friends or lovers or whether it means being cool at a business meeting or in the school classroom or university lecture hall. This shows us how the meaning we give to emotions is a complicated matter, as complicated as learning to use a language. In many cases, we can see how the social settings where emotions are felt and observed can set the social rules on how emotional or how cool we are expected to be both with ourselves and with others. All of this points to the social nature of our feelings and emotions; what we make of the emotions we ourselves are feeling and what others make of us is something we learn in our interactions with others.

In many societies today, many say that we are asked to be fully aware of what we feel and that many of us have become skilled at which emotions to control and which ones to express. A business guru, Daniel Goleman (we first mentioned his book in Chapter 1), calls this "Emotional Intelligence." It refers to the ability of many people today to know about their own emotions as well as to know others' emotions too and to do this skillfully and in different social settings like work and home, intimate relations, and work-a-day relations with others. In these ways, emotions are social and belong to culture.

Competent leaders, for example, are persons who are, among other things, Emotionally Intelligent, referring to the ability of individuals to understand their own emotions and those of others, to discern between different feelings and to label them correctly, and to use emotional information to guide one's own thinking and behavior.

What you just read is a quick summary of some of today's ideas about emotions and their cultural meanings. All these things make up today's "emotional culture." To add something else to this argument, I will point out that the meaning of emotions in one society can change over time, as it happened throughout US history. This also means that the culture of emotions can change or be different among different groups in the same society, such as social classes (rich vs. poor people, upper-middle-class people vs. lower middle-class people, or between different regions of one country where people's cultures—ideas, traditions—can also be different.) I think that these differences are a fine topic for a group discussion.

Based on this argument, we might ask, "What is the source of disgust or fear or anger, say, between Republicans and Democrats in the US today?" Can we explain some of the profound differences between these two groups as differences in their social classes? Can we explain these differences as related to different emotional cultures? A quick answer is Yes we can. But I leave that debate up to your group discussions.

Let us now return to the argument about emotions and culture changing in the same society. So, for example, the culture of my paternal grandmother, Elizabeth Marie Doyle—born in 1877 in Ireland and emigrated to the United States in 1895—is not likely to draw from the same emotional culture I myself draw from today in 2023. For example, as a poor woman (lower class), an immigrant coming to the United States at age 18, she may not even have talked about her feelings and emotions as freely as I do. If I could speak with her today, I might even find out that she did not have in her vocabulary a word for "emotions," especially because she lived before psychology and psychiatry became such an important part of our twentieth- and twenty-first-century world in the United States (More on this point about the rise of psychology later in this chapter). What was important to her, I think, was both her immigrant Irish-Catholicism and what others close to her—especially men like priests, brothers, and her husband—told her about what she felt or was supposed to feel about growing up and being a good wife and mother.

Emotional cultures often teach us which emotions we can express and which emotions we are expected to be silent about or to deny altogether. In the seventeenth century, for example, early modern cultures (like the religion and faith of US Puritans) fostered a silence or reticence about what people were feeling about many things—like about being hungry, feeling pain or discomfort, feeling passionate about a person, and being proud about something one had done. Whereas today, many of us are taught that we should be open about our emotions and taught that we should speak openly about what we want, whom we love, or even that we are jealous of someone. Yet these standards too can vary even today, depending on where we are in society, I mean the *status* we occupy (e.g., our social class and our economic resources, race/ethnicity, and/or our gender or sex identity); these can shape the expectations we and others have about being emotional. Some people today, for example, are more or less constrained in the ways they are able to speak to others about their emotions in the workplace and even with friends.

That emotional cultures have changed over time may certainly describe modern Western cultures like the United States and other parts of North America or the UK or European countries. The cultures of these particular nations, based on histories, tell us that their cultures developed over a long span of time known as the modern era (discussed in Chapter 2), covering the 500-year period from the seventeenth century to the twenty-first century; this span of 500 years was consequential in changing the medieval world into the modern world of industrial capitalism with its cities and moving populations, its increased levels of goods and money, and its new and changing technologies. These modern cultures continue to change today as these modern societies change. One social philosopher called this slow but tumultuous centuries-long period of change and transition, a Long March, writing about the centuries from 1600 to the twenty-first century.

All of these changes are related to today's emotional cultures, since today we live close to modern science and to the practice of psychology to guide us and instruct us about our emotions. Going back to my grandmother who died suddenly in 1942 at age 64, we can consider that she had no science of psychology and no therapy to guide her or to instruct or teach her about emotions. In all likelihood, as a young immigrant girl from Ireland, she turned to prayer, to priests, and to women friends and relatives, including her own five children, to instruct her about her own feelings and emotions. And she undoubtedly learned or was taught to distrust these feelings, thinking that too much emotion was a bad idea and, on the whole, she was taught that feelings and emotions required both self-discipline and personal self-controls.

Today, as Elizabeth's granddaughter, I have new and different ideas about whether emotions are to be trusted as guides for living. On the whole, today's culture urges me to value emotions and to be Emotionally Intelligent and to trust what my emotions tell me about myself and others too. With my feet planted firmly on the ground (an American and pragmatic standard for living), I am expected to be realistic about my emotions and everything else I think and do; to do this is to consult a doctor or psychologist about my feelings and emotions; they will guide me in the best ways to live, I am told. This is because an adult person today is expected to be fully aware of one's emotions and feelings; if one has emotional difficulties or conflicts one should know that about oneself and consult someone about them. This is one of many standards provided (imposed, perhaps) by today's emotional culture in the

United States; namely that people know about their emotional life, monitor it as best they can, and ask others for help with it if needed. In other words, emotional cultures include who the best authorities are with respect to what we feel, whom to consult, and who are the best guides for living with our emotions and our emotional conflicts.

In the section that follows I will briefly describe today's emotional culture. This is a good topic for discussing questions like these: Can you give examples of today's emotional culture? Do you agree or disagree with my argument? Why?

Today's Emotional Culture

1. The Value of Strong Emotions: Being and Acting Emotional

On the whole, emotional *experiences have become so important to many in the US today we can even say that emotions and emotional experiences have become central to what it means to fully be a "self," a real or an authentic self that we strive to know.*

Having strong emotions is also a standard today for evaluating other people, not just ourselves. Emotions serve, at least for many of us, as personal resources from which to claim an identity (Yes! That's who I am. It feels right!) and to build a self-conception. This idea and feeling—about who I am—has become the subject of a book on emotions today, arguing that emotions are vital and practical resources for us living in a rapidly changing world, resources in our relationships, politics, the workplace, leisure, and in our digital interactions too. If emotions are close to who we think we are today, emotions also connect us to a wide range of social issues; emotions are also a vital part of any pressing social issue today from politics to business and advertising and childcare. Issues like immigrants and abortion are clearly intensely emotional, as the positions we take on them are intensely felt; they are close to us.

Here is one example that supports this idea; it is from a recent *Morning Joe* TV news program on MSNBC in New York City in early 2023 (I paraphrase what was said):

> Donny Deutsch, the business and media and branding guru, said that US pollsters today need to ask people much more about what they feel on various political and policy issues. Many polls go wrong or are unhelpful because they fail to do this.

An early statement about today's valuing of strong emotions came from the US social psychologist Guy Swanson. Describing "today" in 1989, Swanson observed that "strong feelings" are beginning to be seen, by many people, in positive terms; emotions today are seen as something real and authentic for people's identities. In other words, today's emotional culture views the self as an emotional self, as a being in touch with one's own emotions and expressing these feelings too. Summarizing these arguments: today's self typically refers to a person whose strong emotions "speak" to her about who she really is and wants to be (authentic). In other words, my emotions and feelings are keys for unlocking my real and unique identity today. Why is this? I do not know for sure, but it may be because we believe that emotions are *natural* aspects of ourselves; they are real and belong to the natural or organic realm.

Here are some of the reasons given for this turn—an "emotional turn"—as some people refer to the growing importance of emotions and emotionality in our current social worlds today (I will provide you, in Sources and Further Readings, with readings on the "emotional turn" and each of these topics that follow). Some reasons given for today's "emotional turn" include these four:

1. The *growth and popularity of psychology and therapy in the United States*, fostering people's emotional awareness.
2. The *changing forms of capitalism and consumerism* in our time; some researchers even claim that capitalism is becoming more emotional than a century ago (through the current values of having fun, pursuing pleasure and greed, and finding in all kinds of ads the idea that people want to display themselves to others). These changes in capitalism and markets began in the United States in the 1950s, the post-war years. Emotions and emotionality grew in these decades, which saw the rise of consumerism and affluence in the United States.

For example, we can see the appeal of strong emotions in the worlds of buying and selling where both stuff and people have "brands" or marketable identities; *what things make us appear sexier and more beautiful or manly?* Put differently, stuff today is supposed to make us excited or happy. Or, doing things like gambling or vacationing is supposed to bring experiences of happiness and pleasure. How about having a lot of crazy fun, like those actors in the TV ads for online gambling apps? Advertisers today and yesterday have worked to appeal to clients' *emotional experiences*.

The issue of pursuing and feeling *authenticity* is also raised by business gurus today in order to sell us stuff or to make us feel good about ourselves, make us comfortable, and/or build feelings of confidence. Writers in US business and commerce today describe the importance of "branding," "branding authenticity," and "emotional connectivity" for consumers of goods and services (see authenticity topic in Chapter 4).

3. Today's *growth of leisure and consumption*, together with the growing pleasures found in play and having fun; the values of having fun and experiencing pleasures both give us permission to be more emotional. In fact, in today's world, pursuing fun is something we are asked to accept as an important and worthwhile way to spend our time, both our worktime and our free time.

4. *Everyday life has become more emotional as it has been shaped more and more by digital messages and pics and videos; these media produce an uptick in our feelings and emotions* (like desire, anger, and anxiety). Increases in the sheer number of digital forms and devices also have this effect, whether those small screens on phones or tablets that we carry with us to work or that we put in our cars or those huge screens at home or those even larger screens in public places like stores and stadiums.

Some further comments on #4 on media. Today's media gives us new tools for our interactions with others ("Did you see that post by Carol? Sooo stupid!" or… "Did you read the text from Pat today?") But the media is also an entirely new *environment*—some say that this new environment is a new *entertainment environment*—restructuring what we do and see as it turns our pursuits of fun and pleasure-seeking into a consistent focus of our daily lives. To facilitate this, there is a messaging service now called WhatsApp that lets users of mobile phones (androids or iPhones) or personal computers (Mac or Windows) call and exchange texts, photos, and video messages with others worldwide and for free.

In other words, our relations with others and our daily routines are increasingly *mediated;* we use and draw from them as we receive and exchange images and stories from TV, emails, texts, Instagram, Twitter, Facebook, and so forth. In fact, it is difficult to think of anything we do today that's untouched by *"mediation."* Watching TV, using the internet, or checking our phones, or listening to a radio are *mediated* actions, meaning that the things we do are shaped by what we see and hear on cells and other devices. These experiences are mediated, since using various gadgets we receive messages from people and from organizations who we will never meet or know directly.

Today, these common experiences do not even require that we listen or watch from specific locations anymore (like from living rooms or cars). Messages, movies, and other images called "memes" come to us in our everyday lives via many different digital technologies and devices like smartphones, iPhones, and tablets, making us more emotionally involved with the photos, videos, events, and dramas we watch or hear in our everyday lives.

Memes are those images or pictures or cartoons that tell entire stories, like Trump's images of himself in jail or of Hillary on the debate stage with him in 2016. Memes are transmitted on the internet, whether via text or email or social media sites. There are many meme sites (I counted, 10–20), websites including Trending Memes, Funniest Memes, Memes of 2020, Today's Memes, and so forth. There is even a site called "Emotional Memes."

Briefly stated, emotions are not only more important today in the ways we relate to each other but how we see the world and what we call "reality." Today's forms of entertainment—entertainment is key!—promote even further the value we place on emotions and feelings as they promote pleasure-seeking, fun, and excitement in venues like movies, sitcoms, videos, and the TV commercials we watch in our everyday lives.

Emotions like intense anger and resentment are also familiar to us as part of today's politics and political movements, what we watch, as much as how intensely we ourselves feel today about politics and policies—race, immigration, gender roles, and sexual identity. All of this intense and regular stimulation draws us in, offering us promises of more to come in the future.

Before moving on, I want to say that I am *not* suggesting any single cause for the growth of emotions in our culture. I am not saying that our new digital worlds alone have changed people. Nor do I claim that psychologists have changed our lives and our institutions, teaching us how to live a good and healthy life. Rather I am trying to see all the different and many forces that are making us more emotional today, in comparison to our forebears.

The rise of psychology, to cite one important example, has certainly made us more emotionally aware and has taught us about "emotions," and this has intensified our emotional quests. But the increased number of therapists and psychologists today—growing first in the 1940s and 1950s—is also *an effect or result* when big changes of modern societies make people more confused, dislocated, and/or anxious about today and tomorrow. So we might say that *psychology arose as an effect* to fill a modern need for people today to deal with their increased changes and conflicts and their neuroses and anxieties. But psychology at the same time also fosters or even creates in many of us an increased knowledge of our own feelings and emotions. So the matter of what comes first—therapy or emotional awareness—and what causes what is a complicated one, since both explanations are undoubtedly, if partially, correct.

These are complex and fruitful topics for readings and discussions to help us sort these issues out: Are we, for example, more individualistic than even our predecessors and cut off from others and society itself? Or are we today more conforming and more like each other than our ancestors were? And how does this fact (individualism vs. conformity) create changes in our behaviors and our emotions? Are we more connected to each other today or less connected than our predecessors? How is this related to our emotionality?

Today's Emotional Culture

2. It's Good to Feel Intensely and to Get Closer to Everything and Everyone

And what about the growing high standard of *emotional intensity* today? Some claim that "intensity" is a vital feature of today's emotional culture. For example, this idea has been proposed by sociologist Daniel Bell. His idea of the "eclipse of distance" is described as a distinguishing mark of culture today. What it means is *that distance or separation is no longer valued as it used to be. Rather, today we value getting close to objects and others, in the games we play and in the dramas and movies we watch, and in the ways we enjoy what we do.*

"Eclipse of distance" *describes an urge or a yearning built into our world today, one that marks a transition from an earlier culturally ideal separation or distance between persons or between persons and physical things to a new standard of closeness.* This earlier standard was what the sociologist Max Weber identified with modernity's "rationalism," its fostering of the value of separation or detachment between people, between people and events, and people and objects in their social worlds, between scientists and the people they study.

This older standard of rationality, during nineteenth-century capitalism, not only operated in all modern institutions and bureaucracies and its forms of authority. It was also an important cultural standard maintained and enacted in the *distances* between individuals, between groups, between spectators and actors, between authorities and us, and so forth. Ask my mother or grandmother: people like these women did not reach out and touch things and people as we do today. In fact doing so was strongly discouraged.

Bell asserts a major transition in our time to a new and emergent cultural standard of *close interaction of selves and objects,* whether between persons or between persons and physical sites like theaters, churches, and museums. This current standard means that today a value is placed on *getting close to others and to things, to "eclipse" or to remove the distances of hierarchies, to rid the world of formalities.*

This account of changing cultural standards and behaviors can be used, for example, to describe *spectators and performances where various dramas on stages draw audiences in as parts of performances* or where museums engage visitors to participate in exhibits, exhibits they came to see. This is clearly a mark of our digital age and its capacity to draw more closely together both individuals and groups, to show and to invite viewers to sites once regarded as private, like bedrooms and dressing rooms, dugouts and locker rooms, and other backstages. In the past many of us got used to these private or secret or forbidden sites being removed from our view or we got used to our exclusion from other sites of interaction like hospital wards or operating room or the dressing rooms where models prepare for Fashion Week displays. By contrast, today's valued disposition is to grasp and to hold things, to bring them close to oneself, to touch and to fondle them.

This idea of *eclipsing distance* is also found in a well-known essay on mechanical reproduction in the modern age, written by Walter Benjamin. a famous social philosopher (see below, Chapter 3 Note 4): "Every day the urge grows stronger to get hold of an object at very close range" and this idea, in this essay, is directly linked to the disappearance of *aura—the value of an original*—in our time when copies are all around us, in the form of photos of things and people or prints of the Mona Lisa, or copies of famous statues by Michelangelo.

Eclipse of distance, the concept, allows us to describe and to interpret what it means, for example, to examine the changing historical features of interactions and relations today, in contrast to older forms that were far more formal and emotionally restrained, at least by our standards today. Put simply, our worlds today are replete with informality, a kind of closeness, a closeness or informality—in our dress (so-called tees and leisure wear) and it is in our speech too (we use first names and some of us drop titles like Sir, Miss, or Doctor)—a closeness also when spectators-as-participants replace spectators who stood or sat at a distance from what they watched. I am thinking, for example, about spectator-participants attending dramas today in theaters, or going to art galleries, or going to parks and public spaces as spectator-participants when we attend memorials to the dead or to victims of violence. I am also thinking of the closeness of strangers via media, interacting online with others we never meet; one sociologist calls these "indirect relationships." One media guru has described these online persons that we relate to as "media friends," those with whom we believe we have both "intimate knowledge" and "emphatic [emotionally close] connection," pointing to the feature of intensity that these mediatized others evoke in us.

One sociologist has called these changes "informalization" and notes that in many countries worldwide, we rarely find today references in etiquette books to social "superiors" and "inferiors." This older distinction once formed an important part of etiquette books for hundreds of years. It disappeared altogether during the course of the twentieth century as statuses were dropped and people increasingly used their own emotions to regulate the ways they interacted with their "social equals." This required an even greater sensitivity to one's own feelings and emotions so that emotions could operate more effectively as skillfully used instruments. These changes—sometimes called "permissiveness" or "informality"—have occurred throughout the world.

As I have argued here, "eclipse of distance" offers us an *image and idea of closeness* as a cultural value today, one that opens up to us new ways of understanding, new standards that replace older ones in our culture and interactions with others today:

- *changes in the ideas of private and public* so that seeing people's backstage regions like bathrooms, bedrooms, and dressing rooms—appeals to us and does not embarrass or disturb or threaten us;
- *new ways of belonging to others and to groups, like* when we feel that we belong with others like us, what we call our identity;
- *of making public spaces our own, making them into places* for one's own pleasure, for play, for politics, or *owning* public places as places for grieving and for mourning our losses or those of others. Sometimes sidewalks and the sides of roads and highways—public spaces—are used as places for us to mark violent incidents.

At this point, I want to ask the reader, maybe as a topic of discussion, "Is closeness also at work in new forms of criminal behavior?" like cases of persons stalking others? Is closeness also found in the various meanings of our pathologies like "social anxiety disorders"? Is closeness-as-a-value present in our sometimes compulsive sharing or showing of intimate stuff to others on our phones or online sites? Do these examples point to changes in the very *meaning of events* once viewed as private, changes occurring in so a short time?

One sociologist has argued that "closeness between persons" is today's "reigning belief," our idea of a "moral good." The standard of closeness can effectively intensify our relations with others; perhaps we find it operating in those events and dramas that appeal to us as participants, like at Broadway musicals or museum shows where actors invite us to participate, or even when we go to highway or sidewalk shrines built to honor accident or crime victims whom we do not really know.

Concluding Thoughts: Culture and Emotion

Emotions are best studied using the concept of culture to understand the social meanings of peoples and things in a particular lifeworld. This approach brings culture and "cognition" (knowledge, or what psychologists mean by cognition) into our understanding of what emotions are. The idea of "emotional culture(s)" draws from this socially shared or collective understanding, using it to study the exact ways that social life matters in what we know and think about emotions. Emotional cultures include some of the following concepts and ideas:

1. "Vocabularies of emotion" or the rules governing a group's ways of expressing the various meanings that emotions have;
2. Emotions operate as signs or signifiers for they communicate and signal things about self and society in the larger sense of a shared culture or in the immediate, situational sense of two or more people interacting;
3. Studies of today's emotional culture integrate some of these common themes:
   (a) today's value of *subjectivity* and *experience*;
   (b) today's shared meanings about identity and people's emotional experiences; emotions are a vital and important aspect of what a self is today; our feelings and emotions, we typically believe, contain our deepest truths and realities;
   (c) the increasing intensity of social life today together with the increased speed of life and the cultural value of closeness.

The most important feature of today's emotional culture(s) is the important value we place on persons' *experiences*—including, of course, our emotional experiences—experiences about reason, facts, and science.

Intensity of feeling has also become a motive for our actions, showing us what we believe is most real today. Our experiences and emotions—what we experience and what we feel are even more real to many of us than our institutions. Put differently, today our *identities and our emotional experiences* possess the quality of Reality, a reality found in our preoccupation with *authenticity, what is most real about who we are.*

What remains to be studied is how this emotional culture operates today in social life, especially in economics, in work, and in politics. Today we can ask whether today's emotional culture and its valuing of personal experience helps or hinders our current institutions like our nation-states, our families, our institutions of faith, and/or our beliefs and practices about the law and its enforcement (our courts and trials, our Supreme Court and its decisions).

Will our emotions, as some argue today, carry us away?

Will emotional experiences and pursuits be rendered far more important than the beliefs we hold in common with others?

Will our experiences take over the world by changing present forms and practices of citizenship and governance, equity and law, marriage and family, markets, and the workplace?

These are the questions I leave you with. It is important what you think.

Chapter 4

THE AUTHENTICITY OF
EMOTIONS TODAY

Let's call this the Age of Authenticity ... something has happened in the
last half-century ... which has profoundly altered the conditions of belief
in our societies. ... We now have a widespread "expressive" individualism...this seems to have become a mass phenomenon.
—*Charles Taylor, A Secular Age*

Life, authentic life, is supposed to be all struggle, unflagging action and
affirmation, the will butting its blunt head against the world's wall...
John Banville, The Sea

The belief that the organic is the chief criterion of what is
authentic in art and life continues ... to have great force
with us [...] the machine is felt to be inimical to the
authenticity of experience and being.
Lionel Trilling, Sincerity and Authenticity

Authenticity, Yesterday and Today

Authenticity is a way of looking at ourselves and other people, an ideal and a
standard of what a person should be today and how we are to achieve it and
to live up to this standard. Authenticity is about being real and honest about
who we are and what we are, first to ourselves and then as we engage with
others. Authenticity involves judging people's feelings and emotions against
this standard, as being real and authentic or not. The expression "Get Real!"
shows us, in ordinary speech, this standard that people are supposed to be;
we are supposed to be Real and not act as if we are living in a dream world or
fantasy world! We are also expected to engage *realistically* with others and to
be real while immersed in the Here and Now, a difficult standard to be sure.

Authenticity is also an important part of today's *modern and contemporary
culture of emotion*—originating in the late eighteenth century, as part of social

and literary movements collectively called Romanticism (dated roughly from the 1790s to the mid-nineteenth century). It was then that *feelings and emotions* became, for the first time, understood as one of *the most vital and real and natural things about ourselves* as human beings. The period of Romanticism was also when "authenticity"—the cultural standard and belief—entered our lives— first as a cultural ideal, and later as a vital and real way to assess others and ourselves. Accordingly, *emotions are believed to be natural and the most powerful and real and truest aspects of ourselves-as-authentic.*

In fact, many of us say that emotions—what we truly feel and allow ourselves to feel—is an important part of who we really are and should strive to be. This is another important meaning of "authenticity," *to be in touch with our feelings and to express them as a real part of us, whether alone or with others.* To act authentically means to lack pretense or to be "real," to be "grounded," to be mentally and emotionally stable. It also means to be who we are naturally and with consistency, not who we are as social beings. Authentic selfhood is never changing; it is a difficult and high standard to achieve for it sets the person against society and its conventions.

Many of us today find the outer world of institutions and roles to be a domain of inauthenticity, of phoniness, unreality, or artificiality. Role-playing is believed to be self-destructive and, even, fraudulent. Instead, we are supposed to enter a journey of self-discovery in pursuit of our real or authentic or essential selves. In modern terms, the authentic self draws from this experienced division between an outer and inner self, between the true inner self and the *persona* or mask that one wears outside. In fact, today the real or the naked self is the self that has torn off its social masks.

Authenticity, the personal ideal, asks us to explore its complexities, by ourselves or with a guide (perhaps a therapist or a guru of our choosing or an online Authenticity Mentor), and to discover deep within ourselves our greatest truths about ourselves, our authenticity! To live an authentic life is to be faithful to this discovery and to live up to this discovery in our relations with others and with the life we choose to live. The pursuit of authenticity is a lifelong pursuit. It is also a difficult one, an unending struggle. But its discovery can be a moment of intense emotions, as described by the famous psychologist Erik Erikson this way: "Feeling deeply and intensely alive—these are moments and experiences that say to us, 'This is *me*! This is who I *really* am!'" Another account from psychology today urges us to live an authentic life that is faithful to our feelings and emotions. If we do this, and do not strain to please all those others, we build confidence in ourselves and evoke in others the type of integrity we possess, one that makes others trust us.

Another related idea is that authenticity today can be called a particular *language of the self,* an intensely sentimental (i.e., suffused with emotion) way of thinking and speaking; authenticity is a way of speaking about who I am, my *identity*, which in its modern form is an intense experience and pursuit of myself as I truly am. Authentic selfhood is how we often think of nature itself, as an organic or natural reality. But there are other aspects of myself—my social self—that are as changeable as the wind: how I am around others and in the many different social situations where I follow roles and rules on how to act in this or that situation. To be authentic means to possess a real and grounded self, not the self of changing situations and acts, presentations, and impressions. The real or grounded or authentic self is like the ground or the earth, symbols of stability and strength. To be inauthentic or ungrounded means to be too easily influenced by others and situations or your environment. Inauthenticity is to be a person who changes who she is around others, even close and intimate others. For this reason, authenticity also means to follow our own dictates, our own experiences and emotions, and not the dictates of society or the social roles we play in everyday life.

Authenticity and the Inner Self

The sources of authenticity and its pursuit lie *deep within us* and exist in a realm outside of society; we discover these sources of the self in many ways, perhaps in meditation or when we "experience" nature or take a yoga class and try to recapture our oneness with nature itself. This is our standard today: to be real and true to ourselves and what we are. We think of this standard as important to pursue as we make our way through everyday life. Authenticity is, in these senses, an effort to capture that wholeness that was lost through modernity, whose material world fragmented us and alienated us from ourselves and from nature itself.

In order to pursue authenticity, it is important to consider ourselves as having these *inner depths* to explore and *an inner voice to hear and heed closely*. Many have written about this idea and experience as important to our quest for authenticity: to be authentic is to think about and listen to this inner self, this private self. This private self is experienced as *more real than the outer self*, that domain of worldly activities and preoccupations. This idea also draws from the idea that there are experiences and emotions that we can distinguish as real ones versus unreal ones, ones that make us, perhaps, either madmen or neurotics; they are really ours but need fixing. And the way to fix them is to live up to them, face them and not deny them, and live the struggle we call "the authentic life."

This view of an inner self is a reversal of the older and ancient view where the life process was ruled by external realities or forces, such as divinities and laws that gave us human beings the order of the universe and its eternal laws which rendered our lives coherent and meaningful. In the old order of things—before modernity—human beings reached outside themselves to find order and meaning, whether from the power of God's grace through the Church's sacraments or by contacting divinities or saints through religious rituals. People communed not only with a single God but also with living holy men and women and/or with saints and angels. Today we reach inside ourselves to discover within us the realm of nature and reality; here is where our truest or authentic self resides. *The voice of Nature and God is now within us.*

This modern disposition called *inwardness* is also a disposition that has attached us, relative to other peoples and civilizations, to *ourselves*, an argument made first by Alexis de Tocqueville, in the mid-nineteenth century, writing about democratic individualism. The sociologist Emile Durkheim elaborated it later in classic works of sociology, particularly in his 1893 study of the industrial division of labor. As Durkheim noted, the modern *cult of the individual* turned people inward. Here are his words (Sources and Further Readings will provide this source for readers):

> There is indeed one area in which the common consciousness has grown stronger ... in its view of the individual. As all the other beliefs and practices assume less and less religious a character, the individual becomes the object of a sort of religion. We carry on the worship of the dignity of the human person which, like all strong acts of worship, has already acquired its superstitions ... It is indeed from society that it draws all its strength, but it is not to society that it binds us: it is to ourselves.

Put differently, the modern self is directed to a field of new objects—objects that exist in a new social space, a world of *inner objects*, objects whose meaning and significance hardly existed before the seventeenth century, that age of sentimentalism when modern "subjectivity" and its "culture of interiority" has been traced. With the eighteenth-century feelings and sentiments became known and pursued, turning the self inward to a domain where nature ("the voice within") speaks to us, as the philosopher Charles Taylor has written about the seventeenth century:

> Sentiment is now important ... because undistorted, normal feeling is my way of access into the design of things, which is the real constitutive good, determining good and bad. ...The modern view ... endorses nature as the source of right impulse or sentiment ... Nature as norm is an inner tendency; it is ready to become the voice within, which

Rousseau will make it, and to be transposed by the Romantics into a richer and deeper inwardness.

Modern persons live with a sense, sometimes conscious but more often unconscious, of their sense of inwardness and freedom, of having a mind and a psychology or psyche, of possessing my unique feelings and emotions and my unique experiences as my very own possessions. In the modern era, historians and philosophers have spent a lifetime tracing when it was that the importance of experience and emotion came together with a love of Nature and of Nature's vitality; many have traced this new understanding of the authentic and emotional self as part of Nature itself, nature within. This new Romantic understanding of the authentic self places great value on a person's freedom and autonomy, its capacity for self-reflection and self-exploration, and its powerful belief in the importance of feeling and sensibility.

At the turn of the nineteenth century (actually later, 1811), Jane Austen published her famous novel, *Sense and Sensibility*, engaging with debates of that time about *sensibility* (the sympathetic actions involved with a person's or a character's feelings) as she told a story of the two Dashwood sisters, Marianne and Elinor. Austen treats these two sisters as representations of sense and sensibility and as a struggle of opposites: Elinor is sensible and reserved; Marianne is the highly expressive and emotional sister.

In this novel and in others of the period, men and women are rendered "autonomous" beings: possessing the ability to have a hand in who and what they were and would become. Human identity is something that modern people increasingly view as an artful process, a sense of personal autonomy, meaning the freedom to act on their own, independently of others and of society itself. *Autonomy* today refers to people's experiences of themselves as relatively independent beings, as centers of knowledge and consciousness, as vital sources of decision and action. This is, in fact, how people in our own time today view selfhood: modern societies are "individualistic" insofar as what modern persons are and what they do are valued in these societies. Of course, autonomy and self-exploration are conditions for persons to pursue an authentic life, to impose a shape on themselves, and, in this way, to control their idea of who and what they are. This is what modern selfhood *is*: modern societies are "individualistic" insofar as the actions of individual persons are among their preeminent values.

Returning to its history, in the late nineteenth century, authenticity—in works of fiction and in other works of art—is portrayed as a struggle against all that society stands for, especially money, fame, and power. At that time, authenticity became a frequent theme of modern literature and art. Authenticity was seen as a search for personal honesty in the face of a civilization that had become an alienating force, a foreign and oppressive force, driven by technology and by the imposition of reason and science in every facet of life, a world dominated by material things and the transforming force of money, an economic energy that was seen to change everything into something it was not.

A related theme of this period was that humankind itself had been changed, an idea clearly expressed by those who argued that all human relations had been changed by the material and productive forces of capitalism. In works of social philosophy of this period (e.g., works by Marx, Kierkegaard, and Nietzsche), humankind was believed to have lost its way, the world was found to have been emptied of meaning, and human lives were devoid of passion and intensity. Consequently, in works of literature by the late nineteenth century, authenticity is represented as a heroic struggle against the (inauthentic) forces of a society owned and operated by the property-owning classes (Marx's "bourgeoisie"). Authenticity, then, grows out of an urge to be free of all imposed social circumstances.

Authenticity can also be portrayed through its opposite, inauthenticity. Gustav Flaubert's famous novel, *Madame Bovary* (1856), is, perhaps, the earliest portrait of a conforming and highly sentimental woman who lives above her means to escape the ordinariness of life in the provinces. She is often viewed as the epitome of inauthenticity. The novel is considered by many to be a great work of fiction, a first work of realism, a book that is clearly concerned with the accurate representation of a person's thoughts and emotions rather than of external events and things.

During the middle to late twentieth century, the idea of authenticity changed dramatically. It is then that we begin to see authenticity as shallow self-deception—Theordore Adorno's "jargon of authenticity" or Christopher Lasch's "culture of narcissism"—a surrender to the dictates of popular culture, mass psychology, and their promises of pleasure and self-actualization. Authenticity-as-jargon, today's "psychobabble" or "pop-psychology" is a kind of cheap or easy authenticity worn on one's sleeve or in one's buttonhole; it listens not to itself but to the dictates of a material and vain civilization held in place by its therapeutic culture of self-promotion.

Whether authenticity is viewed as an escape from the prison of a material civilization or as a kind of selling-out or material entrapment, theories of authenticity have taken as their problem *the pursuit of inner truth and meaningfulness in a social world where possessions and money have taken on a newly found magical power.* Marx called this power of things "commodification." Today our collective wish to be free from material civilization (in this age of performance and of consumerism) has a lot to do with our striving for authenticity. Money and stuff are what inauthenticity breeds and our anxieties about our own authenticity are fueled by this fleeting conviction that brings us back to the early Marx or the Young Marx of 1844 (*The Economic and Philosophical Manuscripts*) where a person's life is threatened by having. This too is a theory of how industrial capitalism threatens human life itself, a theme found in literary works of the nineteenth century.

Authenticity is always a type of self-knowledge, especially a self-knowledge that allows us to disentangle the true from the false self, the real self from its made-up self. The authentic self, a real self, is a person much like the down-and-out character played by William Powell in the classic 1936 Hollywood film *My Man Godfrey*, a man who gives up fame and fortune to live a life of honesty and caring. In 1999, this 1936 movie, *My Man Godfrey*, was deemed "culturally significant" by the US Library of Congress and selected for preservation in the National Film Registry.

Concluding Authenticity

I want to conclude with some recent exchanges with my students—valuable exchanges—who have told me that emotions are the most real thing about us. Quite remarkably, they tell me this in courses and in readings that have almost nothing to do with emotions and identity. To put this conviction of theirs into academic terms, terms most familiar to me: *many young people that I know and read and listen to believe that emotions are the closest thing we have to "nature" and to what we are without social influence.* They also think that emotions are the "real-est" thing we can know about ourselves; they also say that they are fully aware of how much society influences each of us. But, despite social influence in many places today, these young people believe that their feelings and emotions remain relatively untouched by social influences. For these reasons, they tell me that emotions are the closest parts of them that are real and natural. Of course, I tell them that these ideas they have about emotions are *beliefs*, part of culture, their culture. We talk and argue a lot about this. I tell them that they are turning emotions into absolutes. They tell me that I think that everything is social. And they are right in saying that.

In our talking and arguing I can report that both participants—me and them—thoroughly enjoy these discussions, because, after all, we belong together in our belief that emotions are important and that emotions are, in important ways, our very own, an idea of not so long vintage in the modern West, as Charles Taylor has argued. And so we can get excited and emotional in these intensely felt conversations among relative strangers in a public classroom. This intensity does not happen to the same extent in any of our other exchanges and disagreements.

Of course, when my students speak of the reality of their emotional selves they are also telling me about their beliefs about the importance of emotions, of being emotionally real and "authentic," a theme I have written about here, arguing that today's self-identity is close to the idea of authenticity and to the pursuit of reality and the idea, advanced here, that emotions today have become central to our quest for what we call authenticity. It is a culture, our culture, whose origins can be traced to our Romantic past, where feelings and emotions speak to us about who we are, telling us the most vital things about ourselves. Authenticity, in a nutshell, is a way of speaking about who I am, my real identity, an intense experience and pursuit of myself as I truly am. In the words of today's online Urban Dictionary: Authentic means "Being who you are, listening to yourself and making your own decisions, rather than buying all the crap society foists on you. Keep it real."

What is most important about *authenticity*, it seems, is the idea of a real self versus a made-up self. Authenticity, then, is about finding out something about *who we really are*. This authentic self is something natural and unchanging, something, we believe, that is difficult to discover and to hold onto. This authentic self is central to our modern culture today, especially its preoccupation with artificiality and the many things we know to be made-up, from photos and the movies we love to watch to the things we buy and consume, clothes, cosmetics, vacations, cars, furniture, and so forth. Somehow this modern world tells us that we are more than this. We are Real. We are Authentic. The journey to discover our unchanging Reality is worth the struggle. I believe this and so do my students.

Chapter 5

TODAY'S EMOTIONAL PURSUITS AND THEIR MARKETS

Public life today is filled with people who—whether individually or collectively—are engaged in acting emotionally and with intensity. It is as if people have been given a kind of permission to act this way. I do not mean to say that they are only *acting* this way. I think that they are also *feeling the way they act* or, maybe, they are *trying to feel this way*.

I hope this book has provided some tools for thinking about today's emotionality. To make myself even clearer: I have not argued here for a principal or single cause of these changes; rather, I argue that various changes—some more than others—have also changed the ways we experience both emotions and ourselves; these changes have also changed how we feel and act emotionally. Yes, I have been arguing that our world today is more emotional than in the past. I used the concept *emotional culture* to study this change over modern times (over the hundreds of years since, roughly, 1600).

Our most recent changes in emotions and emotional behavior took place since the 1970s when others were identifying certain new features of today's global societies called *late-modernity* or *high-modernity* or *postmodernity*: the terms include changes like the globalization of markets and the rise of new information technologies and service- and knowledge-based economies; changes like these also saw the rise of new cultures of consumption, leisure, and pleasure and the emergence of new digital environments on big screens and small hand-held digital devices. These are the contexts, as I argued, in which our emotional lives today have assumed their contemporary meaning for us, seen especially in the ways we talk and think and act today. *All of these factors*—like, our new digital world and its gadgets, our ways to consume stuff, and our lives on social media—are important parts of the changes taking place in us emotionally. But, as I have said, no single factor has brought this about. Rather *many sources*—like TV shows and ads, social media sites, better techniques of taking photos and videos, and internet shopping and sharing—are parts of the big changes taking place in our social and emotional lives. Let me try to paint a picture of today.

In contemporary public life we witness unprecedented collective displays of emotions in the rise of spectator sports and their mass consumption by fans, in the intense and even violent displays associated with rock and rap concerts, in emotions provoked, displayed, and manipulated during assemblies and political conventions and campaigns, in the rise of new forms of public monuments and memorials called "shrines to sentiment," and in the building of new museums to mark and to remember assassinations, atrocities, and human disasters, like the rise of Holocaust Museums in Dallas, Washington D.C., and Berlin, the Oklahoma City Memorial & Museum, and the NYC 9/11 Memorial and Museum. These very public cultural forms and spaces are visible to all of us but neither studied nor interpreted as important new emotional cultural forms, like today's many internet sites, social media platforms, digital shopping venues, and the videos, pics, and music to go with them; these are new emotional cultural forms too, since they never existed until our recent history, also called The Digital Age, born in the 1970s.

These new sites or cultural forms like the 9/11 Museum and Memorial were designed with the new digital technologies in mind so that publics can "attend" and "tour" them digitally, providing spectators/participants with a constant parade of people, images, voices, music, and sounds to offer us pleasure and other forms of stimulation (or its promise). Of course, these sites also foster new ways for us to remember and to mourn the dead.

Today's digital universe includes the TV ads and talk radio shows we tune in on or stream and those global franchises, accessed anywhere and everywhere via the internet, like KFC or Kentucky Fried Chicken, McDonald's, Century 21 Real Estate, and Hampton by Hilton. Today, we also live among TV "Reality" shows (like The Real World, Survivor, Big Brother, and Judge Judy) that offer us *real people* and *alternative lives*.

Then there are new forms and sites of consuming goods and fun, called by one sociologist, "landscapes of consumption," like the infamous Las Vegas Strip; these places offer us pleasures and delights while shopping at immense malls, gambling on our phones or at the new casino parks, vacationing at theme parks, and eating at theme restaurants, where we choose themes and their "feel" over service and food, like Beaches (the Surf Bar), or spots like Kinky's Dessert Bar on Manhattan's Lower East Side, or Dreamland Roller Rink in Brooklyn, NY, describing itself an "an immersive roller disco experience."

Today's emotional environment is one where psychology's language or discourse, its spoken words, and its written texts (books, newsletters, blogs, etc.) have become a common form of everyday speech and thought, one where emotions and feelings are the topics of endless talk and on radio and television shows and commercials, on Reality Shows, and in the offices of practitioners whom we seek for advice about our "emotional lives"; these ways of think-ing and speaking and acting are also found online using our cell phones and tablets.

In everyday life "emotions," as we say today, are "out there," as important things—if invisible to the eye—that matter and that draw our efforts and our attention, emotions have become things of such value that an entire science is given over to their investigation (psychology), and a virtual army of prac-titioners (clinicians and therapists) exists solely for their skilled manipulation and, if we're lucky, the humane application of these clinical skills. Most of us today are now expected to be Emotionally Intelligent (see Chapter 3). This is how most of us "know" about emotions, in what we see, and what we become part of too. It is a media-generated and media-driven knowledge that forms the backdrop for our more public emotional displays.

As I have already said, in this Digital Age, mass media has become an important part of everyday life and of many of these emotional pur-suits. Today, our everyday lives are played out against what Todd Gitlin described in 2002 as a "shimmering" background: "images and sounds, emanating from television, videotapes, videodisks, video games," but also portable electronics too, like car radios and CD players, iPods or AirPods, and cellphones that allow for us to be plugged in almost consistently to an environment of images, messages, voices, and sounds to stimulate and to entertain us. Of course, this environment also increases our emotional stimulation.

Media is clearly an important key for understanding not only our everyday lives and relations but is a planned part of the development of many of these new and public displays of emotion, driven by large-screen videos, by digital vs. analog music-production techniques, where we hear new things like "wide music," something that feels wider and more spacious than the original stereo recordings made in studios.

Digitals are also prominent in the risky pursuit of "extreme games" and "extreme sports" in both leisure and competitive sports. I am thinking about websites like everestnewstoday.com keeping audiences and journalists informed of current and ongoing events on current climbs and climbers; or, another example, when leading climbers write bestselling books and become media personalities—one of the first was Jon Krakauer, author of the con-troversial *Into Thin Air* (1996). In the same era, Tori Murden, the first woman competitive rower to cross an ocean in 1999—the Atlantic Ocean on the *American Pearl*. Murden was one of the first competitive athletes who competed while posting messages on her website as her fans and "onlookers" sent mes-sages of emotional support. Another case was Diana Nyad's 2013 swim from Havana to Key West (now featured in a 2023 movie starring Annette Bening), a feat recorded on YouTube. Her 110-mile swim lit up Facebook and Twitter with postings and congratulations.

These examples show us how many different forms of information there are today—forms of imagery (moving and still) like photos and videos; these images are often used as *memes* (discrete units of knowledge, gossip, jokes, etc., like a captioned photo or video or a made-up image like a cartoon, often transmitted on social media)—and come before us on screens as we follow events today. I am thinking now of wars or other types of violence or forms of entertainment. These events—wars and violence—are there to capture our attention, in doing this we become more emotional. Memes are, in fact, designed to evoke emotions.

The world of sports entertainment also shows us our emotional world: the US Tennis Open in 2023 (August 22 to September 10) was highly emotional, even if not considered an "extreme sport" like mountain karting or mountain biking. Since 1987, the US Open has been chronologically the fourth and final Grand Slam tournament of the year. This competition is highly lucrative for participants and their payments have grown most recently, effectively increasing the intensity of the competitors and the sport itself.

Coco Gauff, only 19 years old, was 2023's favorite tennis player and winner; one person wrote of her as the "queen" of the 2023 Open. The victory saw Gauff take home $3 million, a figure that helped boost her season's earnings to $5.5 million and her career earnings to $11.1 million. Gauff's playing style is best captured in her opening gesture, a daring and bold fist-pumping yell, "Come on!" Here is a report from the online *The New York Times* (September 4, 2023, cited below in Sources and Further Readings):

> Fans hurry across the grounds to get to their seats in Arthur Ashe Stadium before her singles matches. No one wants to miss her first fist-pumping "Come on!" or one of her ball-chasing points that go corner to corner, backcourt to net and then back again, and increasingly end with her cracking an overhead smash or with her opponent sending the ball into the net.

Let us keep before us that these intense emotional events also take place within a world of business and marketing. Think of the recent frenzy of Taylor Swift's (Summer of 2023) Eras Tour. At the end of 2023, Taylor Swift's net worth reached a calculated $1.1 billion, according to Bloomberg Business News. Again, as reported online (*The New York Times*, online September 5, 2023): "In a summer of tours by stars like Beyoncé, Bruce Springsteen, Morgan Wallen, and Drake, Swift's [Tour] stands apart, in numbers and in media noise." She is also described as a production genius: "She is the best C.E.O., and best chief marketing officer, in the history of music," said Nathan Hubbard, a longtime music and ticketing executive who co-hosts a Swift podcast (*The New York Times* online, September 5, 2023).

More than one article and the online Amazon ad for *Taylor Swift's Little Book* highlight Swift's seeming closeness with her fans fostered by her positive emotional words and lyrics and her emphasis on feelings. Swift regularly defends the underdog and criticizes all discriminations (highly compatible with today's *Zeitgeist* for today's young folk, among others). Here are two excerpts from the Amazon ad for *Taylor Swift's Little Book* that proposes Swift's emotional appeal:

> From her girl squad to the Swifties to the world at large, Taylor's the BFF [Best Friend Forever] of the pop music world. As the go-to shoulder to cry on and chronicler of heartbreak, she relates her personal life and experiences in a "dear diary" style in her music, but the artist is even more popular than her hit songs. One of the most followed on social media, she is a defender of the underdog, open about her feminist and pro-choice views and frequently speaks up against sexism and LGBTQ discrimination.
>
> This collection of Taylor Swift's relatable, inspiring and hugely optimistic quotes and lyrics reveals a caring, generous personality who is all about "the feels" and following your dreams. Sparkling with positivity and feel-good vibes, Taylor is always there to give you the best advice and lift you up when you're down—she's your own personal cheerleader.

The (Loud) Sounds of Today

Let us talk about today's loud sounds, like music concerts or otherwise. I am interested in this because it has long been established that important connections exist between sound and emotion, as well as noise and emotion.

Here is one article documenting louder noises today versus yesterday: In a 2019 article in *The Atlantic Magazine,* we read about a guy called Karthic Thalliker who had recently moved to Chandler, Arizona. The bothersome noise he was hearing came from a server (a computer or system that provides resources, data, services, or programs to other computers over a network) in his town at a company called CyrusOne. As described in this article, noises are more and more a part of the fabric of our lives.

> ...[S]oundscape has been overpowered by the steady roar of machines: a chorus of cars, planes, trains, pumps, drills, stereos, and turbines; of jackhammers, power saws, chain saws, cellphones, and car alarms, plus generators, ventilators, compressors, street sweepers, helicopters, mowers,

and data centers, which are spreading in lockstep with our online obsession and racking up noise complaints along the way. Communities in
France, Ireland, Norway, Canada, North Carolina, Montana, Virginia,
Colorado, Delaware, and Illinois have all protested the whine of data
centers. That's to say nothing of what drones may bring. "The next century will do to the air what the 20th century did to the land, which is to
put roads and noise everywhere." Les Blomberg, the executive director
of the nonprofit Noise Pollution Clearinghouse, told me. Noise, having
emancipated itself from the human hand, is becoming autonomous and
inexhaustible. Human noisemakers have to sleep, but our mechanical
counterparts, which do not tire, die, or strain their vocal cords, can
keep up a constant, inescapable clamor.

But can sound and noise translate into intense emotions? In this book, I have
already described how branding (Chapters 2 and 3) is vitally important, especially to late capitalism, its marketing and consumerism. With the idea of
sound branding or "sonic branding" we can learn how the sounds we hear can
stimulate our emotions and intensify what we feel and even what we believe
too.

Dr. Sol Marghzar is Director of Audiology at Stephen Arnold Music in
Dallas, Texas, a world leader in the field of "sonic branding." In this research
publication, he offers us information on brain science, neurology, and emotion so we can evaluate the connection of emotions to sound branding. With
"sonic branding" we can learn how sound can stimulate our emotions and
intensify not only what we feel but also what we believe.

> Good sonic branding stimulates an emotional response, but great
> sonic branding does more–it becomes rooted in the belief system. It's
> what makes the best sonic brands so deeply resonant and meaningful
> why, when we hear the Mission: Impossible theme, we feel danger in
> the air. Sonic brands, as they tap into our emotions and gradually and
> consistently become beliefs, are irresistible. For brands, they are a gold
> mine.

Musical Sounds Stimulate Identity and Belonging

An online interdisciplinary book collection addresses how it is that musical
sounds can help create in people feelings of belonging or ostracism: I paraphrase the book's introduction:

*Music can and has served people's identities, by engendering feelings of belonging or
alienation. This two-fold function is music's double-edged sword. Music can promote*

feelings of belonging as it sets up boundaries between groups. Music both feeds or engenders belonging, and it can create feelings of not belonging too.

So, whether it is the music at a Taylor Swift concert or at a Holiday sing-a-long or at the recent US Open Tennis Tournament when we heard "America the Beautiful," sung by baritone Will Liverman and played by the Metropolitan Opera Orchestra, we have intensified our self-feelings while, simultaneously, feeling intensely that we *belong* to those we stand or sit with. Liverman's genius includes this *New York Times* critic's statement, now on Liverman's website: "... he balanced forceful intensity with ... intimate singing." Perhaps this phrase is our very own key to unlocking today's emotional culture: we crave intense feelings while knowing that these feelings are our very own precious possessions.

I would like to add here that the mega-success, cultural and economic, of singer-performer Taylor Swift, her Eras Tour or her movie of that tour, has been attributed by some to Swift's uncanny ability to sing and speak to us in intimate or highly personal terms, as if the words and songs are meant for each of us alone. In other words, *soft yet intense intimate experiences, our very own,* make up our most vital *language of the self* today. And Swift knows how to deliver them! These feelings draw us in and give us validation while holding out to us promises of affirmation and future discovery.

But there is more. I refer to a brand-new way of construing self and society, our very own, one that seeks to overcome—to "eclipse" or to wipe out—distance and separation between subject and object (see Chapter 3); in this specific case, to overcome the separation of the viewer/fan and the object or person/performer experienced. Today's media culture disrupts the order of things. For it rearranges space (foreground and background) and beckons spectators/fans to engage as participants in the song or the act, to engage in emotional dramas of affirmation and discovery. In this specific sense, we are all performers today. Here is an insight from a young woman who always wanted to sing and dance throughout her life, like in a musical show:

> Musicals allow characters to express themselves in ways we wish we could. If you feel sad, sing about it. If you're in love, perform a nice duet. If you're involved in some light gang warfare, follow the lead of the Sharks and the Jets and dance dueling choreographed numbers . . . . Musicals may not be realistic, but they are an honest attempt to make sense of life [today]. On stage, characters sing the thoughts they'd never say. Their world is different from our own, yet recognizable in its dedication to the authenticity of human emotion. In real life, you probably don't work through your problems or celebrate your successes with the help of a catchy soundtrack.

This might explain the emotional intensity of Swifties and other fans at a Taylor Swift concert or movie; as a performer, Taylor Swift invites us to come along with her as she sings and performs. The statement above, about musicals, also teaches us something about today and the pull of emotion as our most authentic experience (see Chapter 4). For as the audience experiences together the intense experiences of Swift singing and performing, they become part of Swift and what she sings. But it is much more than that process of dissolving into the singer and her song, as this commentary shows us:

> The fans or the audience become in Swift's words, *"the main characters in this film."* Taylor Swift effectively tells them, "You are my main characters. You are important to me and what I do up here." The feelings attached to this, give each of us in her audience strong feelings of *identity* and *validation*. Perhaps this is why today's valuing of experience and emotion, our pursuits of emotional intensity—are becoming more and more a vital part of our forms of entertainment and pleasure.

In our world today, *intensity of feeling* has become both a motive for our actions as well as a test for showing us what we believe is most real today, even more real than our institutions; our *identities and our emotional experiences* possess that quality of reality, a reality found in our preoccupation with *authenticity*. Emotional experiences *are* our most authentic and real experiences.

Chapter 6

CONCLUDING THOUGHTS: STUDYING EMOTIONS AS CULTURE

...[S]tructure of feeling is the culture of a period: it is the particular living result of all the elements in the general organization....I do not mean that the structure of feeling, any more than the social character, is possessed in the same way by the many individuals in the community. But I think it is a very deep and very wide possession, in all actual communities, precisely because it is on it that communication depends.

— *Raymond Williams, The Long Revolution*

I conclude with another way to talk about culture and emotions, by introducing a British author who wrote about this topic in his work: his name is Raymond Williams. The phrase "structure of feeling," defined above, was developed by Williams to give an account of people's responses to the social upheavals in English society since the eighteenth century. This period of "decisive change" or upheaval took place in almost all of eighteenth-century social life, in literature and painting, in industry and engineering, and in new customs and institutions. People's creative activities, Williams argued, especially in the beginning of the nineteenth century, included far more than art: it embraced "miracles" of creative skill found in industry and engineering. "These are our poems," the Victorian philosopher and historian Thomas Carlyle said, in 1842, of the new steam locomotives of his day. So, Williams placed the steam locomotive engine as central to the entire culture of the early- to mid-nineteenth century, a fact so life-changing at the time and so often overlooked since then. Today, we might say that it is the internet that has similarly altered our lives by shaping so much of our world, our culture, and our relations, one to the other.

In this book, I intended to show that extraordinary creative forces of media and communication hold out to us in our time a new and different *structure of feeling* from those of our predecessors, living only a century ago, and only now becoming apparent to many of us. As Williams argued, this developing structure of feeling *is* our culture today. It is to be found in our most visible

institutions—in our forms of mass media, in our forms of pleasure and entertainment, in the brute facts of our economy, in our forms of work, and in the
ways of life of our social classes, from rich to poor. But it is also discovered in
our notions of community and nationhood, our beliefs in individuality and in
communal life, and in the meaning of the emotions we feel and those we strive
for in our daily lives with others. Our very own structure of feeling is found in
some of the new collective forms of public life: in entertainment, like our Super
Bowls, our Olympics competitions, our Reality TV shows, in our sites of violence and human disaster whose teddy bears and flowers mark the deaths of
school children. Our structure of feeling is also found in our rock concerts
blared from huge stages and equally huge screens. It is also found in today's
popular forms of leisure like mountain climbing and movie tourism ("Put an
Everest in your life!" or "Ride the streets of San Francisco with Bullitt!").

Studying Emotions Critically

Throughout this book, my main interest is to have the reader join me in this
exercise of examining emotions today in a way that is "critical." This word
means many things. In general, it invites us to examine emotions in a way
that is decidedly different from the current ways we think about our emotions
in our everyday lives, namely, as natural objects that tell us something about
ourselves and as important ways to discover our own authenticity. Instead,
I want to distance us from this perspective (literally, to step away from this
viewpoint), one that we share with others today. I have been trying to invite
you, the reader, to think about emotions as *social things* shaped by culture and
history.

Another way of saying this is to offer the reader a counter-discourse on
emotion, a way to think about emotions differently. So, in Chapter 1, I wrote
this way:

> One argument states that emotions are principally experiences of indi-
> viduals; emotions are something that each of us experiences as our own.
> *The main idea of this book is to talk about emotions differently: our culture shapes
> our emotions in important ways.* Put differently, others and society itself,
> shape and have shaped our experiences, including our emotional expe-
> riences—what we feel, how we talk about how we feel, and what feelings
> and emotions *mean to us*, whether we allow ourselves to express our feel-
> ings or not, and what these feelings mean to us or say to us.

Many of the *meanings* of emotions today have been inherited by us from those
who lived before us, sometimes long ago in the era we call the Romantic Era,
originating toward the end of the eighteenth century in Europe. Or, we can

think of our own society today as shaping our emotions in important ways as our society advances to its new stages of industry and consumerism and its privileging of online platforms: social network platforms such as Facebook, Twitter, Instagram, TikTok, and LinkedIn, where users can communicate with friends, family, colleagues, and others; at sites like e-commerce platforms (Amazon, eBay, and Alibaba), users can buy and sell products. All these online platforms and others encourage us to have fun and be emotional; this is why these platforms are an important part of today's *emotional culture,* shaping us as we perform their tasks of connecting or consuming stuff.

I will describe, as best I can, what I am trying to do here: as a woman living in the Modern Age (Chapter 2), I am a liberal modernist in many things. For example, I view a lot of culture and society as oppressive, even as a form of *tyranny,* as setting too many rules for me and others to follow, and as a coercive social world of institutions that are nearly inescapable. This is something like the view of Lionel Trilling; it describes his thinking when he famously wrote about the many works of the modern age. Many of these things in the arts, literature, and entertainment have, he wrote, an *adversary or opposing intention* whose clear purpose has been to detach the reader from the habits of thought and feeling that the larger culture imposes on us all.

To elaborate: I am a liberal educator and a sociologist who thinks that most people, like me, need and want to be freed from the confines of society and its rules, to free each of us from the culture that often dominates and controls us. To do this we have to know what the rules are. To do this is to make clear to ourselves what the sources of our oppression are and where they come from. This is what I set out to do in this book: *to free people from the tyranny of a culture that oppresses us because it is a culture that tells us what to think and how to act about our feelings and emotions.*

This project, *my project,* is one of distancing ourselves from that culture; it comes about when we can see our emotions as things *constructed* in history and in culture. Simply put, I want to argue here that *emotions are not things in our sole possession or control.* In fact, history shows us that other people and institutions have and do tell us what our emotions are and what they mean. Not only religion and the government do this to us; our experience tells us that parents, close friends, and teachers—among others—try to teach us things too.

What have we been told about our emotions? The Romantics, for example, told us that emotions were real and natural things, not *social things.* The "captains of industry" (capitalists) past and present, who have ruled the economies we live under, tell us that we can be satisfied if we buy stuff and have stuff and that this stuff will make us feel good and even make us better mothers and fathers, for example. The many therapists and clinicians today teach us that there is such a thing as *normal people* and *sick people* and that our miseries come principally from ourselves-as-individuals and especially from our particular histories and our families. Therapists also teach us that they can free us from our emotional sufferings by allowing them to treat us and to pay them for this service of therapy or treatment. Politicians teach us that crime and violence are best understood as something done by the "mentally ill" and that this is not principally a problem of laws or guns but a problem of sick individuals (this position plays into our individualism). These are some of the many ways that we can see how society and culture have shaped our emotions and have told us what we are supposed to feel about many things like money, family, sex, migrants, and so forth. So, as I have tried to argue here, in thinking critically about our feelings we need to criticize others and ourselves; we need to distance ourselves from all these rules and conventions, all these *oughts* and *shoulds*.

The approach to emotions I am calling for is decidedly *sociological*. It does not concede to the psychologist or to the influencer the right to tell us what we feel and are supposed to feel. It is an approach that recalls Emile Durkheim's dictum that sociological analysis proceeds as "a stranger to psychology," at a remove from its assumptions and interests. This means that sociological analysis interprets human psychology from within its own frame of reference—a social one—not psychology's or that of any other discipline. Such an analysis views the shaping of emotions as a social process and the practice of psychology itself as assisting in this process of social control.

I also mean that these precious elements of ourselves and our identities— emotions—are one of the most vital ways that we can know ourselves, but that in doing this—knowing ourselves as feeling beings and as beings with feelings—we are always in continual contact with "society": with *languages of the self* that we inherit from our social worlds; with collective ideas and images of what emotions are and how we are supposed to manage them and control them and express them; and, I also mean by this statement—emotions are social things—that society prompts us and teaches us and rehearses us how we are to think and to speak of emotions: *how much* we should or should not feel, *what* we should or should not feel, which feelings and emotions we should cultivate or those we should control or hide or repress, which emotions we are to keep secret from others and secret also from ourselves, and which emotions we can admit to openly. In other words, thinking critically about emotions and their cultures allows us greater freedom as to what we want to feel and what we make of what we feel. This is because a critical view allows us to step outside and judge for ourselves the *cultural construction of emotions*, freeing us from the definitions and meanings of emotions that are not our own.

To think critically about emotions means many of these things. It also means that emotions may be sources or signs of authentic selfhood, but this critical view also shows us that not all kinds of selfhood are welcomed and embraced by "society." Put differently, we are a people, as Irving Howe once wrote, "entranced with depths," especially our own. But we are not all entranced with the same human depths and emotional complexities of many peoples. Some of our emotional depths get us into trouble and are the sources of ostracism, prejudice, and even violence. These prejudicial and destructive ways are how society manipulates us by trying to control our self-feelings and how it shows the importance of seeing clearly the many ways that individuals and groups have a direct hand in trying to control our emotions and those of others. For example, many people we trust do this through teaching us to hate ourselves or to hate others.

My own idea about emotions—clearly one that is both personal (central to my life in the world for some time now) and professional (the academic topic that I have pursued for many years)—is that emotions are not so much my own as they are given to me from the various life-worlds in which I have traveled. Studying emotions has also taught me how emotions are vitally important as I try to cultivate an identity and how I experience and articulate who I am.

But I principally mean to say that emotions are part of the language I have inherited from my family, my social class, and the world of the United States in the twentieth century and into the twenty-first century where I have lived and belonged—a place with all its emphasis on psychiatry and its tales and lessons of "making it," a place where emotions have also been some of the main characters in my own pursuits of having and getting things, of being and becoming someone. In other words, wanting to be someone and becoming someone on the many terrains of life—intimacy, friendship, family, work, community, and so forth—takes feeling things, wanting things, fighting for things, and believing in things—and all of these are helped by owning up to the emotions I really feel, being honest about what each of us feels about ourselves and about others too. Of course, emotions are social! For my emotions are the stuff that others use against me to conform to what they want of me.

A final note on "method" and "theory." This is a work of "interpretation" not "explanation," an exercise in what the anthropologist Clifford Geertz called the perspective of "interpretive anthropology." It is up to my readers and my colleagues in emotion studies to decide if the interpretation I have offered here is adequate to the subject matter.

In this book, I have offered several interpretations of some of the meanings of our emotions today. I have used various texts to assist me in this task: among them, works of social theory on modern and postmodern societies and identities; treatises and narratives about modern individualism (an important piece of our inherited language of the self); works by emotion scholars on today's *emotional cultures*; and studies of social media and mass media.

I have argued many things here as I try to grasp for you and for myself what "emotions" are today. I have used works of philosophers alongside accounts of celebrities in sports and entertainment. This was intentional, neither expedient nor careless of me. That is because I think that everything that matters to us—the gods we worship, our family celebrations, our movies and celebrities, Bruce Springsteen, Beyoncé, and Taylor Swift concerts, the fast food we love, and celebrity tennis matches we watch—each can show us what we care for by looking at how we use or consume them and talk about them.

In other words, it is not just what some have called "high culture" that matters where "culture" is concerned. It is also what is called "popular culture" that matters too. I also think this is a fine way to operate when our social world is going through huge and momentous changes, as we are now. We really should look at everything as a way to read the temperature and the passions of most of us at any given time.

Let me state this important argument here again: "Culture"—referring to the meaning of things and people and emotions—is highly diverse today, and it is always changing in today's social world. Diversity is one of the important marks of today. Diversity is also an important way to view culture. Culture is diverse, many-layered, and multi-coded. Culture is found in the "formal" institutional sites of courtrooms, art museums, and places of worship; but culture is also found in forms of speaking and writing, in family photo albums, and in romance novels. In these senses, culture is not only thoughts we have; culture is also what we feel and what we do.

I have tried in this book to paint a picture of what a cultural sociology of emotions might look like. My leading idea is that emotions are inescapably part of "culture" (the word implies something unified and whole that is actually disparate and multifarious). Emotions are many things; emotions are studied in the fields of biology, chemistry, and neuroscience. My own approach here is not to deny the importance of these different fields but to argue that whatever else "emotions" are part of the world of history and culture. And since they do not exist apart from "culture," it is a worthwhile venture to try to study them this way. One of the truths about emotions is, then, contained in these exercises of cultural interpretation.

SOURCES AND FURTHER READINGS

As a way to make this book accessible and more easily readable for a wide audience as well as for students, educators, and the many who might come across this little book. I did not want to clutter up the chapters with authors' names, with references and citations. Yet, as an educator-sociologist, I still wanted to provide some sources on the topics I write about in the chapters. These readings will, I hope, provide some works to study and/or to use in discussions—whether at a book club or in the classroom—about the topics introduced in the chapters.

These readings often show authors and works that have shaped my own thinking over time, including works by Peter Berger, Alexis de Tocqueville, and other nineteenth-century writers (Karl Marx, Emile Durkheim, Max Weber, Georg Simmel). The works of the pragmatist philosophers have been vitally important in the development of my thinking over time, especially William James, John Dewey, and G.H. Mead.

I prepared the following sources for each of the book's chapters; sources to advance discussions, not to offer a comprehensive list of authors and sources. When the chapter mentions names or cites authors, I have tried to follow this up in the references offered below. My list of readings follows here, chapter by chapter.

PREFACE

1. The epigraph opening this preface is from the cultural anthropologist Clifford Geertz, *The Interpretation of Cultures* (New York: Basic Books, [1973] 2000). On this writer, see Chapter 2 Note 4 and Chapter 6 Notes 5 and 6.
2. The reference in the preface to the book by Peter L. Berger is *Invitation to Sociology* (Garden City NY: Doubleday, 1963).

CHAPTER 1: I list here some important readings on **individualism** to encourage further reading and discussion:

1. A highly accessible conservative (and controversial) interpretation of the relation of individualism and modernity is by Kenneth Minogue, "Individualism and Its Fate," *The Independent Review,* Vol. 17, No. 2 (Fall 2012): 257–269.
2. A recent and important statement on the modern culture of individualism by the social philosopher Charles Taylor (a member of the democratic left who is also critical of some major features of liberalism) can be found on pp. 305–320 (Chapter 18) of his 1989 book *Sources of the Self. The Making of the Modern Identity* (Cambridge MA: Harvard University Press, 1989).
3. A sociologist, Steven Lukes, has studied and written on the various meanings of individualism: Lukes wrote this up in the *Journal of the History of Ideas,* Vol. 32, No. 1 (1971): 45–66. This essay is called "The Meanings of Individualism."
4. I have often used this classic reading on individualism in the classroom; it is a short essay by Alexis de Tocqueville, the nineteenth-century famous young Frenchman and political thinker, who was one of the first writers to closely examine the importance and what he termed, the dangers of individualism in democratic countries. He wrote this in his now-classic book *Democracy in America* (a work of singular importance and influence, a first statement of its kind, written in the 1830s). This short chapter in Vol II of *Democracy…*is entitled "Individualism in Democratic Countries." It is an excellent and brief starting point that can stimulate discussions, even today. Tocqueville's classic treatise is regarded as an original statement about America as well as the "democratic revolution" of the nineteenth century. The work gives us an image of democracy, its inclinations, character, prejudices, and passions. The book *Democracy…*is written "…to learn what we have to fear or to hope from [democracy's] progress." It is considered a first work on the rise of a new mass society of "individuals."
5. *Bowling Alone: The Collapse and Revival of American Community* (New York: Simon and Schuster, 2000) Putnam's contemporary argument in this now-famous book continues the concerns of Tocqueville that individualism is likely to undermine community involvement and social unity in democratic nations. The argument of Putnam is that individualism might endanger democracy itself, because democracy requires some important practices or collective actions (regular gatherings or meetings, shared media, and occasions to get to know others) that unify us as a democratic nation.

6. Sociologist David Riesman's famous 1950 book *The Lonely Crowd* (New Havan CT, Yale University Press) examines different types of American people—traditional types, inner-directed people, and other-directed people. Riesman argues that as modern-industrial societies advanced and more people worked in large corporations, they adopted a tendency to follow the cues and lifestyles of other people and became more "conforming." In other words, in the twentieth century increasing numbers of Americans left behind nineteenth-century "rugged individualism" and became more conforming to others' ways of living and thinking, shaping corporate life and its culture.

7. Sociologist Frank Furedi in his 2004 book *Therapy Culture* (New York and London: Routledge) describes individualism as a cultural trait where people tend to view many problems, personal and collective, as originating within themselves, just as many perceive emotions this way, as *possessions of the self*. See Furedi's book (Chapter 1. The Culture of Emotionalism, pp. 24–43). This argument can be fruitfully compared to Charles Taylor's (1989) view of how emotions became viewed as *interior possessions* (see Chapter 2 Note 3).

8. Adam Grant is a psychologist who writes about emotions as social. See his essay, "There's a Specific Kind of Joy We've Been Missing," accessed July 15, 2021 (July 10, 2021) *The New York Times* Opinion, Guest https://leadersexcellence.com/anger-management.

9. Online "Anger Management Course," accessed July 20, 2021 https://www.hpowersolutions.com/anger-management.

10. Daniel Goleman, *Emotional Intelligence* (New York: Bantam Books, 1995). See below Chapter 3, Note 1.

11. Peter N. Stearns, "An Emotional America," accessed October 22, 2020. *The American Interest* (January 8, 2018). See also Susan J. Matt and Peter N. Stearns, *Doing Emotions History* (Champaign Illinois: University of Illinois Press, 2014).

CHAPTER 2: On Modern Society or **Modernity**.

1. One of the earliest statements by a sociologist on the topic and concept of **modernity** are those of the late sociologist Peter L. Berger and coauthors (Brigitte Berger and Hansfried Kellner), in their 1973 book, *The Homeless Mind: Modernization and Consciousness* (New York: Vintage Books, 1973. See Introduction (pp. 3–20), Chapter 4 (pp. 97–115), and Chapter 8 (pp. 181–200)). All of the writings of the late sociologist, Peter Berger, have as a central theme, the modern world, its ups and downs, its dark

and bright sides and endeavors and especially the rise of "secular" society and the loss of religion as a major social institution that once provided order and meaning to its inhabitants and shielded them from the chaos and continual changes of modern life.

I also refer readers to Berger's book: *Facing Up to Modernity* (New York: Basic Books, 1974). The Introduction to this book is another favorite reading of mine on modernity; the author writes easily and accessibly about this complex topic. Berger makes a good case on p. 8 for the claim that the making of the modern world or modernization took place as various institutions underwent changes in their economies or the ways of producing their collective or shared forms of livelihood; the biggest changes and the most consequential ones came about through changes in technology, as I discuss here in Chapter 3.

2. In the fields of literature and art, Irving Howe's *The Idea of the Modern* (New York: Horizon, 1967) offers many insights into modern literature and art. For example, his idea that modern culture valorizes revolt and rebellion against established institutions and norms contains many important ways to think about modern life and culture in recent centuries, especially its critical and debunking stance, as well as its many protests and rebellions. Even more important is Howe's idea that modern rebellions must never fully succeed but must remain oppositional or adversarial, since a successful rebellion places modern persons or groups in a dilemma of failing to succeed versus succeeding. Howe leaves us with the question: Are we modern people doomed to accept the status of victim over victor?

3. The well-known social philosopher, Charles Taylor, discusses modern society and its individualism in his *Sources of the Self: The Making of Modern Identity*. (Cambridge MA: Harvard University Press, 1989). See Chapter 17, The Culture of Modernity (pp. 85–302), where Taylor treats the new modern emphasis on sentiment and the new (historically new) views on family and marriage as all-important emotional bonds.

    Reading firsthand (often cited by Taylor) the famous eighteenth-century Enlightenment writer, Jean-Jacques Rousseau, we learn how, in that century, *nature became viewed as something inside us*. See his book *Emile* ([1762] 1979), edited, introduced, and translated by Allan Bloom (New York: Basic Books, 1979).

4. In cultural anthropology, the late prominent cultural anthropologist Clifford Geertz wrote about modernity in his last chapter, "Modernities," in his last book entitled *After the Fact* (Cambridge, MA: Harvard University Press, 1995); this chapter is a favorite of mine as I try to write today on this difficult subject of modern culture and emotion. This is because Geertz does not try to escape the difficulties we have today talking and

writing about this complex topic, the culture of emotions within the modern world.

5. Daniel Bell's *Cultural Contradictions of Capitalism, 2/e* (twentieth-anniversary edition, NY: Basic Books, 1996*)*, originally written in 1976, is considered one of the foremost commentaries on twentieth-century modern capitalism. See below, Chapter 3, Note 7.

6. Secondary sources on the movement known as Romanticism: see Charles Taylor, *Sources of the Self* (Note 3); Peter Gay, *Education of the Senses*. Vol. 1 (New York: Oxford University Press, 1984); Harold Bloom, *Romanticism and Consciousness* (New York: W.W. Norton, 1970); Isiah Berlin and Henry Hardy, Forward by John Gray, *The Roots of Romanticism* (2/e Princeton, NJ: Princeton University Press, 2001).

CHAPTER 3: Emotional Culture(s)

Here are some readings on modern and late modern **Emotional Culture(s)**:

1. The book, *Emotions in Late Modernity* (edited by Roger Patulny, Alberto Bellocchi, Rebecca E. Olson, Sukhmani Khorana, Jordan McKenzie and Michelle Peterie, London and New York: Routledge, 2019) is an excellent source for tracing changes in emotional cultures over time. See Chapter 1, pp. 8–24: "Emotions in Late Modernity" by Roger Patulny and Rebecca E. Olson is highly recommended as a group reading.

The social philosopher who referred to the centuries-long tumultuous changes as the Long March is Charles Taylor in his book *Modern Social Imaginaries* (Durham and London: Duke University Press, 2005), Chapter 1, pp. 3–22.

See the argument about emotions today, captured in the title, an argument made in Marci D. Cottingham's book *Practical Feelings: Emotions as Resources in a Dynamic Social World* (NY: Oxford University Press, 2022). This argument is usefully compared to that of Daniel Goleman (see Chapter 1, Note 10).

Here are some readings on **today's Emotional Culture** and the values these emotions draw from:

2. **On the value of intensity**. A 2018 book on emotional intensity by a philosopher: Tristan Garcia *The Life Intense: A Modern Obsession* (translated by A.R. Alexander. Edinburgh: Edinburgh University Press, 2018). This book is highly readable.

A *New York Times* article, "Gaze and Gasp From Atop Manhattan's Alps," provides four evaluations of high sites for their "intensity." One of these four heights called "Edge" provides this evaluation: "Intensity, As high as it gets." (see *The New York Times*, July 18, 2024, Arts Section, pp. C4 and C5).

3. **On the value of strong feelings**. The American social psychologist Guy Swanson (cited in Chapter 3) noted the new value of strong emotions in the United States in the 1980s. Swanson's article is Chapter One, Part I, of the edited 1989 volume by David D. Franks and E. Doyle McCarthy, *The Sociology of Emotions* (Greenwich CT: JAI Press: 3-32, 1989).

4. **On the value of closeness.** This idea of closeness as a value today is best examined, along with Bell's concept, "The eclipse of distance," (See Daniel Bell, 7). See also, Richard Sennett, *The Fall of Public Mena: On the Social Psychology of Capitalism* (New York: Random House, 1977: 255), where Richard Sennett argues that "closeness between persons" is today's "reigning belief," our idea of a "moral good." Another important source on this idea is Walter Benjamin's much-cited essay, "The Work of Art in the Age of Mechanical Reproduction." In *Illuminations* (translated by H. Zohn and edited by H. Arendt). (New York: Schocken, [1950] 1969): 217-52. On p. 223, we read, "Every day the urge grows stronger to get hold of an object at very close range."

5. **The social process of people becoming more informal.** This idea is the argument of Cas Wouters in his 1992 book, *Informalization: Manners and Emotions Since 1890* (London: Sage).

6. **On "the eclipse of distance" in Daniel Bell's work**. Daniel Bell's *Cultural Contradictions of Capitalism*, originally written in 1976 (anniversary edition, 1996), is considered one of the foremost commentators of twentieth-century modern capitalism. This volume and his earlier *The Coming of Post-Industrial Society* identified the important ways that industrial capitalism changes during the post-industrial society.

7. On the World War II period with the growth of the service sector, consumerism, and the extension of global capitalism: Bell is a critic of postmodernism and…*Contradictions* can be read as a moral statement on the rise of a culture of hedonism in the United States—a culture hostile to the ascetic or disciplined culture of classical nineteenth-century capitalism. It is also a book by a thinker and an aesthete, one with a mastery of fields ranging from art and aesthetics to politics and sociology. In… *Contradictions*, see especially Bell's idea of "the eclipse of distance" (discussed in Chapter 3) on pp. 99–119 of his book.

8. On today's **mediated relationships** described as "indirect" and "imagined" see Craig Calhoun's essay, "Indirect Relationships and Imagined Communities: Large-Scale Integration and the Transformation of Everyday Life." In *Social Theory for a Changing Society*, edited by P. Bourdieu and J. Coleman, 9–36 (Boulder, CO: Westview Press, 1991).

A related idea of "media friends" can be found in the Joshua Meyrowitz essay, "The Majority Cult: Love and Grief for Media Friends," in *Les cultes médiatiques: Culture fan et oeuvres*, edited by Philippe Le Guem, 133–162. Rennes: Presses Universitaires de Rennes, 2002.

9. On **memes**: A. Lonnberg, P. Xiao, K. Wolfinger, "The Growth, Spread, and Mutation of Internet Phenomena: A Study of Memes." Accessed on July 4, 2024, https://www.sciencedirect.com/science/article/pii/S2590037420300029 *Applied Mathematics* (January 17, 2020).

10. Hildred Geertz has written on the concept **"vocabulary of emotion"**: "The Vocabulary of Emotion," *Psychiatry*, Vol. 22 (1959): 225–237.

11. On the rise of the importance of **psychology in our culture**: see books by Eva Illouz (see below notes to Chapter 5, Note 1A).

CHAPTER 4. Readings on **Authenticity:**

1. The opening epigraphs for Chapter 4 include Charles Taylor, *A Secular Age* (Cambridge MA: Harvard University Press, Belknap, 2007); John Banville, *The Sea*. (Hampshire, England: Picador Pan Macmillan, 2005); Lionel Trilling *Culture and Authenticity* (Oxford UK: Blackwell, 2008).

2. The principal books cited and used in Chapter 4 include the landmark and influential, *Sincerity and Authenticity* (Cambridge MA: Harvard University Press, 1971) by literary critic Lionel Trilling; *Culture and Authenticity* (Oxford UK: Blackwell, 2008) by anthropologist Charles Lindholm; *On Being Authentic* (London and New York: Routledge, 2004) by philosopher Charles Guignon. Another recommendation is the edited collection of readings on authenticity, one that draws principally from social science, J. Patrick Williams and Phillip Vannini eds., *Authenticity in Culture, Self, and Society* (New York and London: Routledge, 2016).

3. An excellent review essay on the Lionel Trilling book (albeit from a writer highly critical of contemporary "authenticity") is Peter L. Berger's "'Sincerity' and 'Authenticity' in Modern Society," *The Public Interest*, No. 31 (Spring 1973): 81–90.

4. Erik Erikson's quote is from Erikson's *Identity, Youth, and Crisis* (New York: W. W. Norton, 1968, p. 19).

On selling authenticity:

5. See the book *Consuming Catastrophe* by Timothy Recuber (Philadelphia, PA: Temple University Press, 2016). See p. 13, the author's discussion of the best-selling book, by business gurus, Jim Kilmore and Joe Pine,

on how to sell stuff promising authenticity and the importance of clients consuming the real versus the fake. James H. Gilmore and B. Joseph Pine II, *Authenticity: What Consumers Really Want* (Cambridge, MA: Harvard University Business School Press, 2007). See also Chapter 5, Note, 1C.

6. The newsletter essay by Chandra Mukerji is most useful for group discussions: "The Search for Cultural Authenticity," in *Culture. The Newsletter of the Sociology of Culture Section, ASA,* Vol. 21, no. 3 (2007): 1–2.

The following **topics** were also cited in Chapter 4:

7. **The idea of being attached to ourselves.** See the foremost classical writer, Emile Durkheim, in his 1897 book *The Division of Labor in Society* (New Edition, with an Introduction by Lewis Coser. Translated by W.D. Halls. New York: Free Press, 1997). See p. 122. His famous argument is that industrial society no longer attaches us to a group or society; *it attaches us to ourselves.*

8. Charles Taylor on the **inner self,** see *The Sources of the Self: The Making of the Modern Identity* (Cambridge MA: Harvard University Press, 1989, p. 284).

9. The discussion in Chapter 4 of **Jane Austen, novelist, and her treatment of the new "sensibility"** is based on the Penguin Books edition of *Sense and Sensibility* (edited with an Introduction and Notes by Ros Ballaster. London: Penguin Random House Books, 2014). The book's introduction includes an analysis of Austen's treatment of "sensibility" in this novel (xiv–xvii). Its relevance for a history of emotions is clear: This concept emerged in eighteenth-century Britain and was closely associated with studies of the senses as the means through which knowledge is gained. It also became associated with "sentimentalism" or the exaggerated role of feelings and emotions in the domain of morality, judgments of the good and the bad. See also Michael Ferber's Chapter 2 on "sensibility" in his *Romanticism: A Very Short Introduction* (Oxford and New York: Oxford University Press, 2010).

10. The reference in Chapter 4 is to the famous **Gustave Flaubert novel, *Madame Bovary*** (Translated with an Introduction and Notes by Lydia Davis, New York: Penguin Books, 2010).

11. Reference to **Theodore Adorno** includes *The Jargin of Authenticity* (London and New York: Routledge, [1964] 2007); this is best compared with the book by **Christopher Lasch,** *The Culture of Narcissism* (New York: Norton, 1978).

12. For today's **common meanings of authenticity**, see Authenticity, accessed January 8, 2024, from the online Urban Dictionary: https://www.urbandictionary.com/define.php?term=authentic.

CHAPTER 5: Chapter 5 has emphasized three topics of **change in culture and emotions**: 1. Consumption in late capitalism's economy, 2. the rise of social media, and 3. the internet and its generation of a digital world and the gadgets we use to access it. **The readings below emphasize these three areas.** I conclude this section (4) with citations on **noise and emotion** (4).

1. **Consumption in Late Capitalism**
   A. See the highly accessible book by **Eva Illouz** on "Emotional Capitalism," the two-part process where economic and emotional aspects of the self and of life today shape each other: *Cold Intimacies: The Making of Emotional Capitalism* (Cambridge UK: Polity Press 2004). This book treats three topics: Theories of Capitalism, the Rise of Self-Help in the United States, and Internet Dating.

      See also the introduction to Illouz's new book on "emotions as commodities": *Introduction: Emodities or the Making of Emotional Commodities*, (New York and London: Routledge 2018): 1–29.
   B. Economists and others, like sociologist **Eva Illouz**, single out those changes to capitalist economies that extol emotional pursuits. **Martijn Konings's** *The Emotional Logic of Capitalism* (2015, see citation below) argues that while capitalism today is still principally about markets and profit-making, capitalism also provides deep cultural and emotional cohesion for its inhabitants. In places like the United States, beginning in the post-World War II period, capitalism employed service industries and markets to actively remake the affective structure of the anxious modern subject (see page 99, *The Emotional Logic of Capitalism*. Stanford, CA: Stanford University Press, 2015); as noted, this argument is also advanced by Eva Illouz and her concept of "emotional capitalism" (*Cold Intimacies: The Making of Emotional Capitalism*. Cambridge, UK: Polity Press, 2007).
   C. See also a chapter or more of the book *Consuming Catastrophe: Mass Culture in America's Decade of Disaster* by **Timothy Recuber** (Philadelphia PA: Temple University Press 2016). See p. 13, the author's discussion of the best-selling book by business gurus, Jim Kilmore and Joe Pine (James H. Gilmore and B. Joseph Pine, *Authenticity: What Consumers Really Want* (Cambridge, MA: Harvard University Business School Press, 2007), on how to sell stuff promising authenticity and the importance of clients consuming the real versus the fake.
   D. The idea of **"landscapes of consumption"** is from George Ritzer, *Enchanting a Disenchanted World* 2/e (Thousand Oaks CA: Pine

Forge Press, 2009). The topic of "Landscapes of Consumption" is addressed online, accessed July 15, 2024, J. Michael Ryan's 2017 article, "Landscapes of Consumption," In *The Blackwell Encyclopedia of Sociology*, George Ritzer ed., https://doi.org/10.1002/9781405165518.wbeosc114.pub2.

See also Ritzer, George, J. Michael Ryan, and Jeff Stepnisky. "Transformations in Consumer Settings: Landscapes and Beyond," In *Inside Consumption*, R. Ratneshwar & D. Mick eds., (New York: Routledge, 2005: 292–308).

2. **The Rise of Social Media and Us**
   A. **Todd Gitlin's** important book account, *Media Unlimited: How the Torrent of Images and Sounds Overwhelms our Lives* (New York: Henry Holt, 2002), *refers to* the "torrent" of the digital world swirling around and inside us; this book is an outstanding read.
   B. **Douglas Kellner's** books provide a cultural analysis of the rise and effects of "media spectacles" in our lives today: see *Media Spectacle* (New York and London: Routledge, 2003).
   C. On a similar theme, **Maurice Roche**'s book and articles, like his now-classic, *Mega-events and Modernity* (London and New York: Routledge, 2000), trace from the nineteenth century to today, the impact that Expos and Olympics have had on national identities, on the marking of public time and space, and on visions of national citizenship and international (global) society in modern times, late and contemporary.

   See also Roche's article, "Mega-events, Time and Modernity: On Time Structures in Global Society," *Time & Society*, Vol. 12, No. 1 (2003): 99–126.
   D. **John B. Thompson** has written a classic and prescient book, *The Media and Modernity* (Stanford CA: Stanford University Press, 1995) *on the ways changing communication media change the forms of interaction in modern societies.* See especially for discussion the author's account of "mediated experience" in Chapter 7, Self and Experience in a Mediated World, pp. 207–234.
   E. **David Altheide**'s books (see *Media Edge: Media Logic and Social Reality* (New York, Bern, Frankfurt, Berlin, Brussels, Vienna, Oxford, Warsaw: Peter Lang, 2014) also capture something elusive and vitally important about today's forms of mediation of social interaction (pp. 48–50). His most recent book treats the outrageous and unconventional presidency of Donald Trump *Gonzo Governance: The Media Logic*

of Donald Trump (New York and London: Routledge, 2023), especially Trump's unashamed and skillful use of power-through-manipulation. Altheide puts all of this presidency together, while revealing its "media logic."

F. **Sherry Turkle** is a sociologist who has written extensively about the ways the digital world creates a new social environment for us; her works include four books on digital culture: *Alone Together: Why We Expect More from Technology and Less from Each Other* (New York: Basic Books, 2012); *The Second Self: Computers and the Human Spirit* (Cambridge, MA: MIT Press, 2005; *Life on the Screen: Identity in the Age of the Internet* (New York: Simon and Schuster, 1997); *Simulation and Its Discontents* (Cambridge, MA: MIT Press, 2009).

G. **Max Fisher** has argued in *The Chaos Machine: The Inside Story of How Social Media Rewired Our Minds and Our World* (New York: Little Brown, 2022) for a direct connection between social media platforms and the harm they have wrought; their algorithms make us users more extreme in our feelings and opinions; the companies have also preyed on our frailties and weaknesses.

H. **Memes** and their study: see 'Discussion' in Chapter 3 and Chapter 3 Note 9.

Museums and Memorials in the Digital Age

A. **Edward Linenthal** has written two books on contemporary memorials, the Washington Holocaust Museum and the Oklahoma City Memorial: *The Struggle to Create America's Holocaust Museum* (New York: Columbia University Press, 1995) and *The Unfinished Bombing: Oklahoma City in American Memory* (New York: Oxford University Press, 2001).

B. For the best collection on museums and the **Digital Revolution**, see *Museums in a Digital Age,* edited by Ross Parry (New York and London: Routledge 2009).

C. A widely read essay is by **Edward Rothstein** *New York Times* entitled, "Anecdotal Evidence of Homesick Mankind," *The New York Times,* July 2006, B1. Here is an excerpt: "Museums are morphing. Once they were chroniclers or collectors, gathering objects and facts and putting them on display. Now many have become crucibles: places where a cultural identity is hammered out, refined and reshaped. Along the way they also have become community centers, where a group gathers to celebrate its past, commemorate its tragedies and convey its achievements to others."

3. **The Internet and our Digital World Today: Entertainment and Sports**

   A. Celebrities in sports and entertainment show us how their fame has grown exponentially through the internet and through other media coverage like TV:

   Coco Gauff is a fine example of US Sports Fame, from her win at the US Open in New York 2023. Here is an online article on her games there:

   The New York Times, (September 4, 2023), Matthew Futterman, "This Year's US Open Belongs to Coco Gauff, Win or Lose," accessed December 20, 2023 https://www.nytimes.com/2023/09/04/sports/tennis/us-open-coco-gauff-quarterfinals.html.

   B. Discussions of the recent and intense career and fandom of **Taylor Swift** can be found in these sources, discussed in Chapter 5:

   The Little Book of Taylor Swift: Words to Shake It Off (Portland OR: Orange Hippo, 2022).

   The New York Times article: by Ben Sisario (August 5, 2023), "How Taylor Swift's Eras Tour Conquered the World," accessed August 7, 2023, https://www.nytimes.com/2023/08/05/arts/music/taylor-swift-eras-tour.html.

   On the appeal of Taylor Swift, see also online article by Bill Murphy Jr. (October 14, 2023), "Taylor Swift Just Taught a Master Class in Emotional Intelligence: These 7 Words Mattered Most," *Inc.,* accessed October 15, 2023, *The Newsletter,* https://www.inc.com/bill-murphy-jr/taylor-swift-just-taught-a-brilliant-lesson-in-emotional-intelligence.html.

   I have inserted into the Taylor Swift discussion a highly original newsletter article about the attraction of musicals that helps explain the attraction of Swift. Online at *The Johns Hopkins Newsletter (April 4, 2013),* "The Culture: Broadway Allows a Unique Expression of Inner Emotions Through Song," by Alexa Kwiatkoski, accessed December 15, 2023, https://www.jhunewsletter.com/article/2013/04/the-culture-broadway-allows-a-unique-expression-of-inner-emotions-through-song-36605.

4. On **Noise and Emotion, Chapter 5**

   A. The following articles and an edited collection address the relation of noise or sound and emotion: *The Atlantic Magazine,* "Why Everything is Getting Louder," by Bianca Bosker (November 15, 2019), accessed October 20, 2023, https://www.theatlantic.com/magazine/archive/2019/11/the-end-of-silence/598366.

B. "The Science of Sound," by Dr. **Sol Marghzar** AuD, CA, Director of Audiology, Stephen Arnold Music. Accessed on September 19, 2023, https://stephenarnoldmusic.com/scienceofsound/#:~:text =The%20amygdala%20is%20extremely%20sensitive,provoke %20certain%20thoughts%20and%20behaviors.

C. Online research article: "Six Ways Your Brain Transforms Sound Into Emotion," accessed on September 18, 2023, *Bright Audiology*, the newsletter (August 13, 2015) https://www.brightaudiology.com /hearing-loss-articles/6-ways-your-brain-transforms-sound-into -emotion.

D. Online research article: "Arousing the Sound: A Field Study on the Emotional Impact on Children of Arousing Sound Design and 3D Audio Spatialization in an Audio Story," accessed April 19, 2024, https://www.frontiersin.org/journals/psychology/articles/10.3389/ fpsyg.2020.00737/full by Francisco Cuadrado, Isabel Lopez-, Cobo, Tania Mateos-Blanco, Ana Tajadura-Jimnez, *Frontiers in Psychology* (Vol. 11, May 2020).

E. The edited collection on music and belonging is online at https:// www.cambridgescholars.com/resources/pdfs/978-1-4438-4830-5 accessed July 19, 2024.

The chapter citation is from the Introductory essay by the editor, Magdalena Waligórska ("Music and the Boundaries of (Non) Belonging" in (online book) *Music, Longing and Belonging: Articulations of the Self and the Other in the Musical Realm* (Cambridge Scholars Publishing, 2013: 1–10).

F. Works by **Alex Ross** on noise and sound and emotion, *The New Yorker Magazine* (August 1, 2023): 61–63. "Requiem for a Festival," about the end of Mostly Mozart Concert Series at Lincoln Center, as a subject in the rising disdain for classical music; on p. 62. Ross refers to "the very high sonic level of the plaza music…the sound level of an outdoor dance contest approached 110 decibels." See also an article by Ross that is an extended reflection of what "noise" is: *The New Yorker Magazine* (April 22 and 29, 2024): 22–27. See also his 2008 book, *The Rest is Noise* (New York: Picador Publishers).

CHAPTER 6: What is a **"cultural" study of emotions?**

1. Epigraph from **Raymond Williams**, his term **"structure of feeling,"** is from his book, *The Long Revolution* (New York: Harper Torchbooks, 1961): 48.

2. Clifford Geertz's **"interpretive anthropology"** can be read in his highly influential, *The Interpretation of Cultures* (New York: Basic Books, 1973), reissued in 2000.

3. From an email exchange with **Isaac Ariail Reed**, the prominent theorist of historical and cultural sociology. I asked him about the recent history of using various texts and dramas, both popular and others, to study "culture" (discussed in Chapter 6). I offer these authors and texts (Notes 4–8), suggested by my emails with Professor Reed:

4. The earlier idea of "culture" was that of **Matthew Arnold**, the nineteenth-century poet and critic, or that of **F. R. Leavis**, the English literary critic of the early-to-mid-twentieth century. Both held that authentic culture was that of the educated elite; this was later called "high culture" by Herbert J. Gans. For an essay on a history of these various meanings of "culture" see, Raymond Williams, *Keywords,* revised edition (New York: Oxford, 1983).

5. Clifford **Geertz**'s famous essay, "Deep Play: Notes on the Balinese Cockfight," is reprinted in his book, *The Interpretation of Cultures* (New York: Basic Books, 1973), reissued in 2000, pp. 412–453.

6. Geertz's essay (cited directly above, 5), together with the "new historicism" of **Stephen Greenblatt**, will help us understand this new approach to cultural studies; for example, see *Practicing New Historicism* by C. Gallagher and S. Greenblatt (Chicago, IL: University of Chicago Press, 2001).

7. From the Centre for Contemporary Cultural Studies in Birmingham, England read, for example, **Dick Hebdige**'s pathbreaking book, *Subculture and the Meaning of Style* (London: Routledge, 1979) and read the many works by the distinguished cultural theorist, **Stuart Hall**.

8. **Janice Radway**'s book *Reading the Romance* (Chapel Hill, NC: University of North Caroline Press, 1984). Two authors whose works are related to this reading are now considered classics of cultural sociology, books by Herbert Gans and by Diana Crane.

9. **Modrias Eksteins** has written an essay on the methods and ideas of **Siegfried Krakauer**, "The Rag Picker," *International Journal of Politics, Culture and Society,* Vol. 10, No. 4 (1997): 609–613. This reading is directly relevant to the argument about the use of all aspects of a society to understand its culture.

10. A final note: **A Personal Statement on Studying Emotions as Culture.**

    I would be remiss if I did not provide for my readers something about my own approach to the study of emotions, namely those authors and works that I have drawn from here. I highlight the following as most important:

works by the late sociologist Peter L. Berger on "modernity";

works by the late cultural anthropologist Clifford Geertz;

works by the early sociologist, Charles Horton Cooley on self and society;

works by classic nineteenth-century social thinkers especially, Tocqueville on democratic individualism, Marx on ideology, Durkheim on social solidarity, Weber on the theory of social *rationalization*, and Simmel on the cultural foundations of ideation and emotion and his concept "style of life";

the pragmatist philosophers, especially these two, G.H. Mead, on language and mind; John Dewey on action and thinking;

and these **three contemporary writers**: Jeffrey C. Alexander on drama and on "cultural sociology." Of special attention are the author's arguments in the book *The Civil Sphere* (New York: Oxford, 2006); R.S. Perinbanayagam on the semiotic foundations of thinking, especially the recent *Dialogues, Dramas, and Emotions: Essays in Interactionist Sociology*. (New York: Lexington Books, 2023); and Isaac Ariail Reed on theories of social knowledge; see his *Interpretation and Social Knowledge: on the Use of Theory in the Human Sciences* (Chicago, IL: The University of Chicago Press, 2011).

I am also indebted to the intellectual tradition of "symbolic interaction."

INDEX

www.ingramcontent.com/pod-product-compliance
Lightning Source LLC
Chambersburg PA
CBHW020008290326
41935CB00007B/345